# PLEA OF THE NEGRO SOLDIER

CHARLES FRED. WHITE.

# PLEA OF THE NEGRO SOLDIER

### AND

## A HUNDRED OTHER POEMS

By

### CORPORAL CHARLES FRED. WHITE

*The Black Heritage Library Collection*

 **BOOKS FOR LIBRARIES PRESS**
**FREEPORT, NEW YORK**
1970

First Published 1908
Reprinted 1970

Reprinted from a copy in the
Fisk University Library Negro Collection

INTERNATIONAL STANDARD BOOK NUMBER:
0-8369-8720-9

LIBRARY OF CONGRESS CATALOG CARD NUMBER:
78-133164

PRINTED IN THE UNITED STATES OF AMERICA

# Plea of the Negro Soldier

AND

# A Hundred Other Poems

BY

## CORPORAL CHARLES FRED. WHITE

CHAPLAIN OF WESLEY S. BRASS CAMP
NO. 37, UNITED SPANISH
WAR VETERANS.

PRESS OF
ENTERPRISE PRINTING COMPANY,
EASTHAMPTON, MASS.

This book is lovingly dedicated to my mother and sisters, whose every prayer has been for my success.

The Author.

# CONTENTS.

5

7

# PREFACE.

To all who may perchance peruse the pages of
   this book
      These lines are written.
To all who may misunderstand their meaning
   full these lines
      Are dedicated.
To those of studious nature who are wont to
   criticise
      They are submitted.
To those whose comprehension will allow them
   to enjoy
      They are dictated.

To those whose curiosity may cause them to ob-
   tain
      This book to read it;
To those who in their lonely hours would be
   consoled awhile,
      Or who may heed it;
To those who love to read the inmost feelings
   of a soul
      Lonely and blighted;

9

To those whose hearts are kind and good and
    who with simple things
      Are much delighted;

I recommend these unkempt lines with pleasure
    and good will
      To entertain them:
These murmurings of ill content and happiness
    combined
      With love of nature,
Encompassing the remnant of ambitions, cir-
    cumstance
      Of which restrained them
From measuring their height, yet have not their
    persistence lost
      Nor temperature.

*Charles Fred. White.*

# FOREWORD.

If you had been deprived of an education in your early youth; if then you had run away from home to obtain that education and found, after some ten or eleven years of knocking and being knocked about, that you could not save money enough out of your scant earnings to pay for your schooling; if, during those years, you had traveled through nearly every state between Boston and San Francisco and from Virginia, Tennessee and Arkansas to the southern part of Canada, being compelled to work, generally, in menial positions if you wished to keep from starving; you would not think you had been very fortunate in life.

If you had walked the streets of a great city by day, sometimes with only five cents in your pockets and only a scant meal in your stomach for several hours, and all one December night stood in the archway of a church door to rest from a weary day of job hunting; if you had lived upon scant means, compelled to support yourself, often being physically hungry in an endeavor to satisfy your mental hunger for knowledge; if, again, you had been compelled to leave school for a year or two because of lack of means; you would think that yours was indeed a hard, rough lot.

If your dear, grayhaired grandmother, whom you had taught to write while yet you were a child in turn for her reading, self taught, the Bible to you, had told you how she was cruelly sold from her mother and sisters while but a mere girl and that she had never again seen any of them; if she had pictured to your infant mind, while tears came stealing down her cheeks, the inhuman beating and torture administered to her and her fellow slaves by her "Christian" masters; if she had bared her arm, her back, her breast, and showed unto your childish vision the cruel scars, the heritage of all her life of bonded toil, which she would bear until her death; if she had afterwards told you how beastly, how shamefully, how disgracefully she had been treated by those Caucasian brutes, who distorted the Holy Word into sponsor for their crime; if your grandfather had described to you as you sat upon his knee the indignity and torture heaped upon him and his while he was a slave; if your own mother and father, born in slavery, had related to you the insult, wrong and injustice meted out to them after the war by their *good white friends* of the South, which they had left never to return; you would hardly feel that any folk but black folk were your friends.

If you had served your country in the ranks of the volunteer army in foreign war, when that country did not protect your life, nor even your property, at home, when you could not be sure that upon your return you would not find that some friend or relative had been despoiled of life, liberty or property without due process of law; if you had afterwards arrived one day in Denver, Colorado, tired and hungry, and been refused anything to eat in three or four public restaurants, notwithstanding you had offered money to pay for it,especially when you were neatly dressed and well behaved; if you had plodded wearily through the sultry, dusty streets of the business section of St. Louis, Missouri, on a hot summer day, parching with thirst, while not a druggist, confectioner, nor anyone else whom you asked would either give or sell you a drink of water or soda; if then you had walked across the bridge over the Mississippi to East St. Louis, Illinois, and been given a glass of warm dishwater to

13

drink by a man who had been kind enough to sell you a sandwich from his lunch cart; if you had been refused a glass of soda phosphate, to relieve a depression, in a drug store in the heart of Cincinnati, Ohio, (the home of Secretary W. H. Taft) or a dish of ice cream at the gate of the United States Army barracks at Fort Thomas, Kentucky, or if you had been "jim-crowed" in Little Rock, Arkansas; if you had been threatened with lynching by a mob of Missouri whites because you fought for your own rights; if even in many places in the North you had been proscribed, ostracised and mistreated, refused lodging, or recognition which you undoubtedly deserved;—and all this for no other reason than that your complexion is darker than the hue of those who so misuse you,—you would surely think this a wretched and ungrateful country.

So, while reading the poems on the following pages, if you think that sometimes they are too radical or harsh, turn back to this foreword, read it again, and, taking for granted that the author's own experience is here but briefly told and that these writings are based upon actual facts, consider whether they are harsher than that experience. Then consider further that this same

14

person has absolutely no prejudice towards any human being on account of race, color or creed, that he thinks as much of one person as of any other, so long as he is treated well and justly,—for

The soul has no color but of eyes,
Possesses no malice, no disguise:
The soul knows no creed but love and faith;
It knows only man; it knows no race:—

consider also that he lives in harmony with everyone who will be congenial to him; and, after all, ask yourself whether he is not partly right, whether you yourself could love a country and a people who had treated you as herein stated.

C.F.W.

# I THANK THEE, LORD.

I thank Thee, Lord, that Thou hast brought
Me to this age, that Thou hast wrought
Such miracles and wondrous things
Beneath the shadow of Thy wings.
Forever and anon I'll sing
The praise of Jesus Christ, my King.

'Tis Thou who made all things we see;
Thou who hast always watched o'er me
While in the toils of life entwined;
Who ever unto Thee hast bound
Me with thy love, so rich and kind,
And showed to me the way around
All things which blemish or would mar
Thy glory, which doth from me bar
The sinful fiends of wickedness
Which, but for Thee, would me possess:
To Thee do I my glad voice raise;
To Thee I ever will sing praise.

Come, all ye lands and join the throng;
Sing out His praises loud and long;
Walk in the path that He has trod;
Give glory to almighty God.
Come, join with me, and we will blend
Our voices, and we'll heav'nward send,

Hosanna! Thine the glory be
Who died for us and made us free!
*1898.*


## PRAYER.

Lord, our God and Father up in heav'n, we
praise Thy name:
May Thy kingdom holy on this earth e'er be
the same.
Thou art everlasting through all time that is
to come:
Thou art ever welcoming us to our heavenly
home.
Holy, holy, holy Lord, we pray Thee keep us
ever:
Guide and keep us in the right and ne'er Thy
succor sever;
For, though we may think we're strong, we are
yet very weak;
So we lean on Thy great arm the while Thy
way we seek.
*1898.*

# THE SOUTH'S UNGOLDEN RULE,

## OR

# AN AMERICAN RIDDLE.

Contented, he was lured from homeland;
  Free, he has been captive made;
Though human, he was bound in chains and
  Sold like beast in slavery's trade.

Kind-hearted, he was beat and tortured,
  Though resentless, he was killed;
Forgiving, was his wife extorted,
  Forced to yield to brutish will.

Obedient, he was made to labor;
  Faithful, he was starved and scarred;
Deserving, he was shown no favor;
  Handsome, his offspring was marred.

Religious, worship was denied him;
  Truthful, he has been profaned;
Though grateful, white men have belied him;
  Dead, his corpse was torn and maimed.

Progressive, was deprived of learning;
  Though respectful, driv'n to shame;
Though innocent, was lynched by burning:
  Has not of his own a name.

*Sept., 1900.*

19

# JOLLITY.

Ah! You're quite a jolly girl I see,
    Where are you from?
You are just the kind I'd have you be;
    You're full of fun:
Always telling jokes, with pretty smiles
    Upon your face,
Thus you pass away the tiresome whiles
    With ease and grace.


Ha! Ha! Ha! You say you're always gay,
    Content and free?
Well, I know you've been quite so to-day;
    So full of glee.
It is better, I suppose, to bear
    Life as it comes,
Let it go as best it may, and care
    Not when 'tis done.


Life is not of such worth that it ought
    To be the cause
Of a constant worry, making naught
    One's pleasant joys.
Of this short existence we know but
    Present and past:

Future lifts her veil not, lingers not,
    But glides so fast

That no man has ever felt her wrath,
    Nor heard her speak:
So we're blindly stumbling 'long her path
    Each day and week.
Thus we go through life at her behest,
    And we should be
Happy, with a hope some day to rest
    On Future's knee.

*Sept., 1900.*

## MEDITATIONS OF A NEGRO'S MIND, I.

[Read at a mass meeting in the state capitol building
at Springfield, Illinois, 1899.]

Had I a land that I might call my home,
    I would be glad;
But I'm compelled this cruel world to roam
    With feeling sad,
Because the Lord, in his wise way, preferred
    To make me black;
Therefore the lighter races of this earth
    Would keep me back.

Methinks, sometimes, it is a hard, rough lot
The Negro has to bear, willing or not:
He's scorned and driv'n about from door to door
Without an open ear to his implore;
Without a heart's being touched by his sad plight;
Without a hand to help his way to fight,
Save that of God, who doth all things aright.

Two hundred eighty years have past and gone
    Since first he trod upon this unkind land:
Two hundred eighty years of basest wrong
    Pollute this nation's history, to stand
As long as this creation shall extend,
Though not recorded by historian's pen.

The boasted pride sung by this populace,
    The liberty and freedom talked upon
Are not enjoyed by this darker race,
    Although these do by right to it belong.

A flag which doth enshroud beneath its fold
Such deeds of crime unwritten and untold,
Save by the hand and tongue of the oppressed,
Or by a friend,— of whom we few possess,—
Is not a flag of freedom, nor for right,
However long it wave, or to what height.

Yet, such a flag does now wave o'er our head,
Intent our names to hide of martyred dead;

But no; the Negro's tongue shall not be hushed,
Nor his protesting feeling e'er be crushed,
Until the hand of dastard crime is stayed
And bound by freedom's laws, by free *men* made.
*May,1899.*

## MEDITATIONS OF A NEGRO'S MIND, II.

Doth negro claim existence now
Who meek to unjust laws would bow
Without a protest on his brow,
    And call himself a *man?*
Doth live a member of our race
Who dares not coward villains face
To drive them from their hiding place,
    And thus for his rights stand?

Was e'er a dark hued infant born,
In childhood from its mother torn
And reared up in this land of scorn,
    And yet doth love this land?
Was ever slave upon this soil
Contented year by year to toil

While ne'er, within, his blood did boil
  To unshackle his hand?

Did e'er, while this proud nation's slave,
A negro's heart within him rave,
Yet, never he an utt'rance gave,
  And claim right to this sod?
Did e'er Caucasian trade or bart
In human souls with dev'lish art,
Nor once was turned his stony heart,
  And claim to serve his God?

Did e'er one of this paler tribe
Despoil his darker brother's bride,
Defy the law with threat or bribe,
  And boast an honored name?
Did e'er a statesman in this land
Boast of his firm and rightful stand,
Nor tried to loose the fettered hand,
  And claim a right to fame?

*March, 1900.*

# AFRO-AMERICA.

[Read at a mass meeting in the state capitol building
at Springfield, Illinois, 1899.]

Oh Country, 'tis to thee,
Land of the lynching bee,
   To thee we wail.
How long shall these base wrongs
Pollute thy freedom's songs?
To thee the right belongs
   Them to assail.

Our native country, see
How we long to be free
   To live and love.
We long to see the time
When this most heinous crime
Shall change to deeds divine,
   Like those above.

Let wailings swell on high,
Let rocks, trees, hills, all cry,
   "God's will be done:"
Let Christian souls arouse,
Let all our cause espouse
And keep our fathers' vows
   Ere ruin come.

Now, gracious God, to Thee
In Thine all-wise mercy,
    We do appeal:
May this land soon be brought
Out of this doom it's wrought,
For long, in vain, we've sought
    Freedom to feel.

*May, 1899.*

## MEDITATIONS OF A NEGRO'S MIND, III.

I wonder why the Negro should be hated;
    He has done no great wrong unto mankind:
He was out of the same crude dust created
    As all the rest of human race, I find.

He's tried to do the best that he knew how to,
    Although he was oppressed in shameful bond;
Persisted not to do what he should not do;
    To duty's call he always did respond.

*Sept., 1900.*

# A LETTER TO MY SISTER.

Allene, sweet sister, with the blood
Of youth yet coursing through your cheeks,
I was informed, not long ago,
That you had quit attending school.
What is the cause that you should act
So rashly as to stop your search
Through that enormous library
Piled up by Time in ages past
And guarded with unceasing care
By fond Existence?   I wish that
You might know the full value of
An education.   I think you
Would reconsider soon your act
And turn again toward the path
Of learning, and would never cease
To delve into the depths of things
Unthought by others.   I suppose,
Though, that you have considered all
This thoroughly, and have resolved
That 'tis as well for you to stop.
Yet, I cannot but think that you
Have acted wrongly.   Surely you
Will in some future year regret
That you have thought it wise and well
To discontinue the pursuit

27

Of knowledge.  I should you advise
To get all education that
Can well be stored within your brain;
For nothing that you learn will be
Of any disadvantage to
You through the life that is to last
Until your death.  If you have learned
To deeply think upon the things
Brought up in daily studies, 'twill
Help you to think more thoroughly
Into the cares of daily life;
No matter what their size or weight.

I was surprised, indeed, and sad
To hear you had determined thus
To forfeit your good chance to be
In future time a person of
Great wealth in wit and lore of books.

Since I was taken out of school
I've often wished that I might find
An opportunity to go
To school again.  I'd like to have
A college course of quite four years,
Which I intend some day to get,
E'en though I may be then some years
A senior o'er my present age.

When you and Lilian had begun
To study music, you recall
The fact that you cared naught for it,
While Lilian studied much and learned
Quite readily to play: so well
That afterwards you were inspired
With full desire to be equipped
To play as well as she?   Forthwith
You then began to practice much
And study more than you at first
Did care to; so that now you have
Succeeded quite in learning well
To chant the strains of sweetness deep
And melody upon the keys
Of the piano, bringing forth
The deep expressions, beauties and
The symphonies of art and life.

So, in the years when Lilian
Has graduated from her class
At high school, and equipped herself
With lore of books, you will regret
That you did not advantage take
Of time, then past, by draining all
The books in reach of their great wealth
Of countless treasures, precious gems,
And hiding them away within

29

Your chest of memory, to use
At times when they are needed most.
Therefore, I'd be much pleased if you
Would continue your term of school
And finish honorably and well.

*Nov., 1900.*

## THE HOLIDAYS.

T'ward the last of bleak December
  When the northern fields are bare,
When the trees are still and leafless,
  And the frost flies through the air,

When the bluebird has flown southward
  And the robin seeks more warmth,
When wild-goose and duck have had their
  Summer outing in the north,

Then the hare and deer are hunted
  By the jolly city folk
Who have left their toil and business;
  Donned their winter cap and cloak.

30

Then the farmer has his pleasure,
    For the harvest has been stored
In the barns and sheds for winter,
    And the fruit preserved and lowered

To the cellar for safe keeping,
    And the winter meat is cured.
Squirrel, too, has hid his acorns
    In some safe spot and secured.

When the student's mind is wearied
    With the studies of the fall
And the melancholy days have
    Settled calmly over all,

Then begins a week of pleasure
    Known to us as "Holidays."
Christmas Eve is first to greet us
    With its joyous rhymes and lays.

On this night we hang our stockings
    Side by side along the wall
To be filled with toys and sweet things
    By Saint Nicholas, as he's called.

On the next day, then, we get up
    When the sun at early morn
Peeps out on the joys before him:—
    Christmas day, when Christ was born.

All this day we're gay and mirthful;
  One whole week is spent in glee;
Then comes New Year's day with all its
  Vows to be, or not to be.

So the world begins its journey
  Through the coming year of strife,
Mingling all its joys and sorrows
  To compose what we call life.

*Dec., 1900.*


## SONG OF A SUMMER BREEZE.

I have come, as it were, from nowhere;
  I have no cherished home:
I am welcomed by high and low folk,
  Wherever I may roam.

Oft I come, as a gust or soft wind,
  With gentleness and glee;
For a while I will linger, and then
  I'm gone as silently.

Though I come over dismal marshland,
  I bring not its foul air;

32

Though I come from the grave, or death bed,
   I bring not their despair;

Though I travel o'er plain and mountain,
   I bring not weary hours;
Though o'er desert I pass, or rockland,
   I've naught but soft, sweet flowers.

Though the sunlight forsake my pathway,
   My heart seems light and free;
Though the world may be filled with sorrow,
   I bring it not with me.

Oft on cold snowy days I fly through
   The chilled and frosty air,
Causing icicled trees to shed tears
   While worn by winter's care.

In the spring I revive the flowers,
   The trees, the grass; the bird
Sings, the bee and the brook make music
   As sweet as you have heard.

In the summer I breathe on warm days
   And cause them to withdraw
Their intense heat; I make the green fields
   The prettiest e'er you saw.

As I fly through the land, I gather
   The sweetest for my store. —

Oft I come in the sad, still autumn
To soothe some soul that's sore.

I have sorrows and cares and troubles
As deep and great as yours,
But I cover them o'er with laughter,
And bind them up secure

With the chords of delight and kindness,
Then paint them well with smiles
And distribute them to the lonely
To turn away the whiles.

I invade the repose of sick room
And fan the fevered brow.
In seclusion of love I'm list'ning,
To mark the sacred vow.

In the solemnness deep of worship,
In hour of fervent prayer,
Oft I busy myself with wafting
A breath of solace there.

I have come, from where?—From the unknown.
A mystery I seem.
I shall pass, and no man shall see me;
Return but as a dream.

*Feb., 1901.*

# AN EASTER MORN.

Brightly now the sun is shining
  On this Easter Sabbath morn:
Voices heav'nward are inclining;
  And the sky's without a scorn.

Beautiful white clouds are moving
  'Cross the broad expanse of blue
Which o'erhangs the earth, so soothing,
  Reflecting its azure hue

In the ponds, the streams and rivers,
  Lending color to their depth.
In the breeze the dead grass quivers
  As if it received fresh breath.

Mildness hovers in the weather,
  Gently nursing Easter's form
As the rich and poor together
  Nursed the baby which was born,

Years ago, within a manger
  In the far East, we are told.
(Though He was to them a stranger,
  They took Him fine stones and gold.)

Warmth and pleasantness are keeping
  Hand in hand with light and air:

35

Through the sod the grass is creeping:
  Happiness seems everywhere.

Not more perfect in the springtime
  Could a day be than is this,
Stripped of all of winter's cold clime,
  With a touch of summer's bliss.

Yet, with all the joy and sunshine,
  There's some rain beneath the sod.—
Though a life be mirthful, sometime
  Through a dismal swamp it's trod.
*April, 1901.*


## AN INCIDENT

A charming maid got on the train
  With mother and her father,
Bound for the western hill and plain,
  Expecting naught to bother.

But soon there came a trim young man
  Who rushed up to the car,
Excited, with expression wan,
  And asked of me how far

He'd have to go to get some flowers.
  I told him he might find
Some at the news stand.   All his powers
  Of haste he then aligned,

In order to return before
  The time the train should leave;
For at first sight he'd loved her more
  Than she could well believe.

He happened to be at the same
  Hotel where she had stayed,
And when she in to dinner came
  He saw and loved the maid.

He had not met this sweet, French Miss,
  (Now formally, I mean,)
But he had learned her name was "*Thyss*,"
  When he her face had seen.

He found the flow'rs, in haste returned,
  And sent them in to her;
His mind was wild, his heart had yearned
  Her sympathy to stir.

She knew him not, nor e'en had thought
  That she was thus admired.
She was surprised much and was fraught
  With wonder, and desired

To see the person who had sent
　　This token of respect;
So to the vestibule she went
　　And asked his name to get.

I knew him not better than she.
　　Impatiently he paced
The platform along side of me,
　　Until the maid he faced.

He tried to say something to her,
　　But failed; his voice was weak;
His lips uttered a faint murmur;
　　But thus his heart did speak:

*"Comme le ciel est si bleu,*
　　*Pour vous mon pauvre coeur est en feu;*
*Comme mon coeur l'est ce jour,*
　　*Je parlerai d'amour toujours."*

*"Voulez-vous m'accepter?*
　　*Puis-je mon coeur, en fin, vous laisser?*
*Je vous aime, chere mademoiselle,*
　　*Et la, sans vous, mon coeur est frele."*
*May, 1901.*

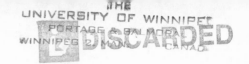
# LOVE.

[Published in the Exeter (N. H.) News-Letter, 1904.]

In the soul is born a feeling,
　　Or a sentiment, called love,
Which is nursed, caressed and cherished
　　With care, tender, from Above.

By the law of God, who made us,
　　By the guidance of its like,
It selects a life companion
　　From where'er its fancies strike.

Often does it make an error;
　　Oft is deceived in its find;
Oft is scorned and turned back coldly:
　　Oft brings sadness to the mind.

By the law of man 'tis given
　　As a trust, with cupid's seal,
To be nurtured, fondly cared for:
　　Thus becomes life's woe or weal.

By the law of changeful nature,
　　It is made to ill agree;
In its haste has oft been blinded
　　By some false identity.

On its whims have hung great fortunes,
　　Or the fates of great careers.

39

By the sting of its rejection,
    Lives have been engulfed in tears.

Hearts have yearned for its fond presence
    E'en grim Death has stayed his stroke
To permit this magic power
    To repair a heart, once broke.

For love's sake have lives been ended:
    From its joy has sorrow fled:
To its care is honor trusted.
    Souls bereft of love are dead.

*May, 1901.*


## ENCOURAGEMENT.

'Tis not winter time yet, my dear heart,
    Though autumn has crept through the air;
'Tis not time to be sad and lonely;
    There's no need to live in despair.

The birds are yet singing with sweetness;
    The grass is yet growing and green.
The streams are yet rippling and merry;
    The snow-clad hills are not yet seen.

40

The flowers are yet full and handsome;
    The squirrel yet plays in the trees;
The sun has lost none of his lustre;
    There's some warmth yet left in the breeze.

Therefore, dear heart, cheer up, be mirthful;
    Throb not with less vigor and vim;
Thy blood flows as freely as ever;
    Thy life is yet nourished by Him.

*Oct., 1901.*


## THOUGHTS OF THANKSGIVING.

Thanksgiving day is coming soon,
    That long remembered day
When nature gives her blessed boon
    To all America.

On that glad day, in all our land,
    The people, in their wake,
Give thanks to God, whose mighty hand
    Deals blessings good and great.

The roast goose, steaming on the plate,
    The sweet potato cobbler,

41

The cranberry sauce, the pudding baked,
The seasoned turkey gobbler,—

All these delights and many more,
From north, south, west and east,
Do all the nation keep in store
For this Thanksgiving feast.

Alas, for those who are denied
This blessed boon of God!
May all the needy be supplied
Like Israel by the rod.

*Nov., 1895.*

## IN HONOR OF LINCOLN.

Hail! ye heroes who yet stand!
Hail the martyr of our land!
Hail him who for his country delved!
Him who the great rebellion quelled!

Him who rent our fetters twain,
Him who broke the clanking chain
Which 'round our lives did e'er entwine,
Resounding loud its doleful chime!

42

On, oh nation, strong and great,
Though the world predict thy fate!
The future may yet have in store
Some deed to test thy strength of yore.

On, oh nation, in thy might,
Ever upward in thy flight!
Hail Lincoln,—though to rest he's laid,—
Who freed us by God's mighty aid.

*Jan., 1896.*

## SPRING.

The day is mild, the spring is here,
The blithest season of the year:
Although the ground's o'erlaid with snow,
The sun sends forth his warming glow.

The trees will soon begin to bud
And, as the sun dries up the mud,
The dandelion may be seen,
With yellow head and clad in green.

The children homeward wend their way,
Some hurry on, some stop to play.

43

Their lessons for the day are done;
From school they march out, one by one.

I see, across yon vacant space,
As through the trees my visions trace,
A dairy wagon with its load
Of milk and butter on the road.

The geese and chickens all are out
And picking at the first green sprout,
As through the shallow snow it peeps,
While warm, spring wind above it sweeps.

I sit within my humble wall
Reflecting over winter's fall:
It seems to me but yesterday
With kingly pomp he held his sway.

*March, 1896;*


## WHAT IS LOVE?

Love: what is love;
That fascinating power, divine,
Which fills the heart with thoughts sublime,
Which causes men to tear their hair,

Which brings delight and brings despair
Into the peaceful mind?

In vain, in vain, I've delved to find,
To fathom from its mystic rhyme,
As down the stealthy roll of time
It spreads its blessings o'er mankind,
Or, laughing wildly at his fear,
Sends down its vengeance, year by year,
The incantations of this word
Which, though I sleep, are ever heard.

Perchance, some mortal who has found
Himself within this magic mound
Of uninvited thought can give
The explanation of this myth
Which has, by its unwonted skill,
Defied the universe at will
For these long years.

*May. 1896.*


## PAST MEMORIES.

As I look on the dreary day,
    From which the warmth of sun has flown,
My thoughts seem wand'ring far away,
    As though past mem'ries back had blown.

Yet, while the day is dark and drear
    And I am sitting all alone,
A thought, which brings to me good cheer,
    Betakes my mind to home, sweet home.

I think of all the loved ones there,
    Of brothers, and of sisters, too,
Of father, and of mother fair
    Who guided me my young days through.

Of grandpa, also, old and gray,
    In Tennessee's far, southern land,
Who toils on sadly, day by day,
    With withered, feebly active hand.

Cheer up, grandfather, and be gay,
    For, though this life to sorrow's given,
You soon will leave and go away
    To your companion, now in heaven.

Life is but a mortal casing
    For the soul while here on earth;
Ever with an eye upraising
    To our Father's heav'nly hearth.

*Feb., 1897.*

# SABBATH.

'Tis a pleasant Sunday morning,
　　And the sun is shining clear,
Ever giving us a warning
　　That our God is always near.

Now a breeze, as though from springtime,
　　Wafts itself from o'er the lake,
Bringing with it all the sweet chimes
　　From the church bells in its wake.

As the golden sunshine cometh
　　Softly through my window pane,
As the rippling water runneth
　　O'er the pebbles to the main,

As the trees, in breezes swaying,
　　Gently bow their heads, inclined,
Seems to me I hear them saying;
　　"Peace on earth to all mankind."

Now that God is in his Glory,
　　Let us praise Him more and more;
Let us sing the offertory
　　Till to Him on high we soar.

*Feb., 1898.*

# PLAY OF THE IMAGINATION.

Hark! I hear the sound of singing,
And of sleigh-bells, gaily ringing,
And the sound of steeds fast springing,
   Fleeting o'er the frozen snow.

Now are cheers and bursts of laughter!
Louder, louder, as though faster,
Thinking never of disaster,
   While adown the lane they go!

Now the sound of horns and jingles,
As a sweet voice with it mingles,
Steals upon my ear and tingles,
   Lingers, while the moon hangs low.

Now the sounds are growing fainter;—
Distance makes enchantment daintier
As the hour grows still and quainter,—
   Till they die away so low,

Scarce I hear them in the distance
While, intent, my strained ear listens
O'er the snow which 'round me glistens:
   Now they're gone.–From memory?–No.

*Feb., 1898.*

# DESPONDENCY.

I care not how soon I leave here;
   Leave this cruel, lonely world:
I've a longing to depart to
   Where the flag of peace, unfurled,

Spreads its grand, celestial tidings,
   As it waves in silence there,
Through the realms of the Creator,
   Far beyond this earthly air.

As I sit within my chamber
   Musing o'er my wasted life,
I can think of naught but sadness
   Intermixed with toil and strife.

All the world about seems joyous,
   Seems to be o'erfilled with glee:
Nature, with inviting glances,
   Bids us all her joys to see.

But, alas! I feel not cheerful,
   Matters not how bright the day,
For my thoughts are doleful, dreary,
   Of the mystic far-away.

Though betimes I may seem joyful
   From some outward look or sign,

Yet, within, my heart beats sadly,
　　As with burden on the mind.

You who read this simple poem,
　　Think not as is here expressed;
'Tis a miserable feeling
　　Thus to be in mind distressed.

*Feb., 1898.*


## WAR'S INSPIRATION.

If God hath willed that I should die,—
And thus our race name glorify,—
While fighting amid war's alarms,
'Mid crashing shells and cannons' storms,
While freedom's flag waves o'er my head,
O'er dire remains of martyred dead
Who gave their lives and lent their aid,
Who faltered not, nor were afraid
To die upon the battle-ground
With unfurled glory all around,
Then, I am full content to die
And be upraised to Him on high.

*Feb., 1898*

## TO LILIAN.

I knew not I a sister had
   With intellect so great,
Who loves all things of nature's fad
   And handles their great weight

With such ease and dexterity,
   Such wondrous grace and skill,
That warm-hearted posterity
   With inspirations fill

When reading o'er her scopic lines
   Of philanthropic trend,
Imbibing what her verse defines
   And what her mind doth lend.

Strive on, dear sister, toward the goal
   And pluck your laurels there:
Though sometimes you be on the shoal,
   Steer out, nor linger there.

*April, 1898.*


## TO H. P. L.

Dear maiden, please accept my thanks, wilt thou,
For this kind token of thy loving nature,

As I in high appreciation bow
Before thy queenly form of beauteous feature.

Thy thoughtfulness and kindness in this deed
I never shall, through countless years, forget;
For, though thou art not of my race nor creed,
Thou gavest me this gift without regret.

The marked simplicity of thy chaste ways,
The welcome glow which beams in thy bright eyes,
The smile which overspreads thy face for days
And weeks alike, make thee a living prize

For whom the members of the other sex
Do well to strive and contrive, day by day,
Endeav'ring, while thou dost their brains perplex,
Each one to make thee his and win the fray.

And I would say to him who doth succeed
That, had he searched o'er all this universe,
He would have found no one to better lead
Him through this world of coldness and reverse.

Thou art a gem of rarity and worth,
Of beauteous manner and of winning grace,
Who captureth the high esteem of earth
With winsome ways and ever smiling face.

Thou scornest not the thought to stoop so low
As to make glad the hearts of sons of toil

Who are around thee going to and fro
About their work, endeavoring to foil

The shirking fiends of laziness and make
Great preparations for commencement day
In which thou art to modestly partake
And with the wings of knowledge fly away.

May all good fortune which great God hath given
And all success and goodness here on earth
Befall thee, and when thou dost reach the heaven
May thy seat be before thy Father's hearth.

This tribute to a heart so great and kind
That 'round itself doth welcome all mankind
I pay thee.   I shall cherish while life last
This fond memento of a day soon past.

*June, 1898.*


## TO THE GIRLS OF KENWOOD.

[Written in Cuba.]

The pretty emblem of good luck,
    Presented by brave hearts to me,
No hand but death from me shall pluck:
    It shall a fond memento be.

A picture of the same appears
 Upon this card of little worth,
There to remain, perhaps for years,
 Until 'tis burned on age's hearth.

*1898.*


# THE EIGHTH ILLINOIS IN CUBA.

[From an essay read before our Sunday School in camp
near San Luis, Santiago de Cuba.]

Camped in Cuba in the mountains,
 Far away from home and friends,
From the precious civil fountains,
 In a land of marsh and fens,

*In this church of thatch and palm leaf,
 Cut and built by our own hands,
We are holding Sunday service
 As is done in many lands.

Far away o'er hill and valley,
 Over marsh and mountain top,
Over battle-ground where rallied
 Man and horse at freedom's knock,

Over ruined mill and city,
 Over waste of richest loam

54

Where the dove of peace once flitted,
    But was driven from its home

By the shells of cruel cannon
    And the swords of treachery,
Fly our thoughts to home and loved ones
    Whom we soon expect to see.

Over barren devastation,
    O'er a land of wasted wealth,
Over what was once plantation,
    But now lies untilled, undwelt,

Far across the stretch of ocean,
    Far beyond the sunken Maine,
Pray our friends in deep devotion
    For our safe return again.

But, instead of tears of pleasure,
    Some must shed their tears for grief,
For depleted is our measure;—
    †Fourteen rest the sod beneath.

No more reveille shall wake them;
    Taps has blown for them its last;
Nor shall ever foe o'ertake them,
    For their fighting all is past.

Comrades, over our departed
    We have fired the death salute;

Let us cheer their broken-hearted
   Loved ones, grieved and destitute.

*Jan., 1899.*

*Mr. White, who was adjutant of the regimental church organization, planned and superintended the construction of this building, which was said to be the first Protestant church on that part of the island. Several Cubans and soldiers were converted here, and a baptising was held in a stream near the camp by Chaplain Jordan Chavis.

†Six others afterwards died of disease or accident.

## THE EIGHTH RETURNING FROM CUBA.

Gaily we ride by the river,
   Rumbling o'er mountains and creeks,
Laughing and jolly as ever,
   With warm, red blood in our cheeks,

Riding through cuts in the mountains,
   Riding through tunnels in hills,
By the fresh, silvery fountains,
   O'er crystal cascades and rills,

Through rural towns and collections,
   Stations of various names,

56

High hills in all the directions,
    Through swamps and pine-covered plains,

Scenery fine of description,
    Beautiful valleys and vales,
Grandeur of wondrous conception
    Portrayed on most gorgeous scales,

'Round curves alongside the river,
    Under cliffs hanging with rock,—
Naught from my mind e'er can sever
    These scenes in memory locked.

By farms of modern perfection
    With their storehouses o'erfilled
With produce, fine for selection,
    From rich land thoroughly tilled,

Through forest and broad plantation,
    Hickory, walnut, oak, birch,
Cities of large population,
    Districts of value and worth;

Thus comes the gallant Eighth Regiment,
    Volunteered from Illinois,
Back from the Cuban intrenchment,—
    Brave band of true-hearted boys.

*March, 1899.*

# THE NEGRO VOLUNTEER.

[Written for the National Standard-Enterprise, Springfield, Illinois.]

He volunteered his life and health
  To go to cruel war—
Increasing thus his country's wealth
  In soldier boys afar—

To fight the battles of a land
  Which does not him protect,
And, though great danger was at hand,
  He did not e'en object.

He went, it seemed, to certain death
  By bullet, sword or scourge,
Where dry, hot trade winds blow their breath
  And rains the land submerge.

He knew well when he left his home—
  Though home it did not seem,—
In Cuba's far off wilds to roam,
  That death raged there supreme;

That Spanish treachery and hate,
  That fever's dreaded ills,
That rain and heat and heavy weight
  While on the march or drills,

Awaited him his fate to seal,
  His life-blood's wall to break,

To laugh in scorn when he should reel
   And fall, no more to wake.

Though monsters such did him confront
   And threaten him with death,
His bravery they could not daunt,
   But made him fear the less.

Of such brave hearts as he does own
   A land might well be proud,
Enforce the laws, protect his home,
   His all, from lawless crowd.

The bird doth soar in lofty space,
   The fish doth swim the sea,
The beast doth field and forest pace,
   The Negro—where hath he?

The bird at night flies to her nest,
   The beast's home is his lair,
The fish in quiet nook doth rest,
   The Negro must despair

Because, alas, he hath no home,
   No place to lay his head
That he can truly call his own;
   Nor e'en when he is dead

Doth his lone grave remembrance gain,
   In hearts, save of his kind;

Nor is it marked by tomb of fame,
    Nor wreathed with flower nor vine.
*June, 1899.*


## A HYMN OF COUNSEL.

[Published in the National Standard-Enterprise.]

To him who knoweth not the value of his life,
    Nor careth aught for that which elevateth him,
Who findeth existence to be a constant strife,
    Who brings upon himself despair or sorrow dim,
I would recite this simple poem of advice
And beg him to accept without return of price.

For, though it come not from most learned brain
        of man,
    Nor may of classic nor of cultured language be,
This simple lay may cause someone to better scan
    The prospects of his being, or more plainly see
The need of education, or of moral worth,
Which two combined bring comfort, peace and
        joy to earth.

I would first say to him: be honest, good and true;
    Be faithful to thyself and value self-respect;
Do all that is within thy scope and power to do
    To keep thyself and others prudently erect;

Observant ever be of great and common things,
And listen to the songs which reverend nature
    sings.

Betake thyself within secluded walls of thought,
    And there, in loneliness, portray thyself to thee,
Arrayed in all thy foolish waste, so dearly bought,
    Which causeth oft thy heart to droop and
        downcast be,
And fathom from beneath this mass of malcontent
Thy better nature which was downward crushed
    and pent.

Then raise it gently up from out its gloomy nest,
    Support it with the strong arm of thy will and
        sense
And cherish it with all the life within thy breast,
    And it will grow so rapid and with glow intense,
'Twill blossom in the springtime of its newer birth
And bid thee pause to view the goodness of the
    earth.

If thou, perchance, should find thee restlessly
    engaged
    In wav'ring contemplation o'er thy changing
    ways,
Dislodge these diabolic thoughts from off their
    stage;

Think not of wrong, but of the beauty of these
 lays.
Beget thee to the avenues of shining light,
For danger lurks about in shadows of the night.

Go willingly unto the fountain of success,
 Fed by the spring of learning, beautified by love,
And drink thou of it freely, that thou may possess
 The mighty power of knowledge, sent from
 Heav'n above;
For education is a wealth of untold worth
Which, once acquired, can ne'er be lost by thee
 in earth.

Full many kingdoms in himself doth man possess,
 The thrones of which are oft usurped by evil
 power;
Grim indolence, the solemn death-knell to
 success,
 Doth lurk about in ev'ry hidden nook and bower.
Simplicity is greatness, born within itself,
And plainly marks all greatest deeds and thoughts
 of wealth.

Improve thy time and talent while 'tis yet in reach.
 Strive hard to grasp a branch of fame's exalted
 tree;
Take heed to that which doth great elevation
 teach;

Mark well each lesson learned, for 'twill of
    value be;
Love thou all things which tend to principle of
    right;
Keep all good deeds of men always within thy
    sight.

But if thou thinkest that thou needest counsel not,
    Or that thou'rt wise enough and strength hast
        to endure
These worldly battles often waged long, fierce and
    hot,
    Heed not the simple words and teachings of
        the pure,
And thou shalt pass into the vast oblivion's doom
Where naught but sorrowful regretfulness doth
    bloom.
*June, 1899.*




## DECEMBER.

The days are short, the air is cold,
    The bleak wind stirs the lifeless trees,
The sun sends forth faint rays of gold,
    While Autumn rests at peace and ease.

63

The summer birds have flown away
   To warmer climes and greener shores,
And little snowbirds chirp their lay
   While picking crumbs from kitchen doors.

The cows are milked within the barn,
   The horses bridled in the stall,
The geese and chickens, to keep warm,
   Stand on one foot, but never fall.

The children, playing on the lawn,
   Are building snow men at the gate,
Or, having done that, they have gone
   Out coasting, hitching, or to skate.

The school has closed for holidays
   And Santa Claus will soon be here
To turn the melancholy rays
   Into a week of mirth and cheer

The present year will soon be past,
   For it is old and feeble now,
And o'er December's bier, at last,
   Must New Year make his reverent bow.
*Dec., 1896.*

# AT EVENING.

Evening sun beams not upon me
    As I sit in silent shade
Musing o'er this earthly dwelling,
    Which to rest must soon be laid.

Ah, my heart grows sad and weary;
    As I'm dreaming, all alone,
Night is drawing swiftly onward,
    And I'm "One day nearer home."

Stealthily the night brigades are
    Creeping o'er the walls of day
To attack him in his weakness,
    Conquer and drive him away.

Soon the hosts of knights of Darkness,
    With their glittering, starry shield,
Will usurp Day's throne and fortress
    And a while his sceptre wield.

Then the gallant Day will muster
    All his forces for the fight
And with light and rays of sunshine
    Drive the foe fast from the site.

*Sept., 1899.*

# A HISTORICAL REVIEW.

In fourteen hundred ninety-two
   America was found
And olden theory proved untrue—
   That earth was square, not round.

In fourteen-ninety-seven, then,
   John Cabot started out,
Resolving straight across to wend,
   And shortened much the route.

In 1506 Columbus died,
   A prisoner in chains,
Although for several years he'd cried
   For freedom from these pains.

In fifteen hundred sixty-five
   St. Augustine was founded,
And ever since has stood and thrived,
   Though centuries have rounded.

In 1607 Jamestown's homes
   Appeared among the wild—
And here begins a tale of woe
   Of this land's orphan child.

In 1619 Slavery's wrong
   Disgraced our country's page

And made a blot so deep and long,
   'Twill last through countless age.

In seventeen hundred seventy-five,
   Oppressed by English law,
The colonists a plan contrived
   To wage a freedom's war.

In 1781 they gained
   The object of their strife;
Ungratefully they tighter chained
   The slave to misery's life.

In '70 brave Attuck shed
   His life-blood in the fight,
The first of all this country's dead
   To die for freedom's right.

E'er since, in all this nation's wars,
   The Negro's played great part,
Glad always to defend her cause
   From depth of his brave heart.

In '65 he fought the South
   To save the nation's name:
An accident which came about
   Freed him from slavery's chain.

Two hundred years, and more, they'd kept
   Him 'neath this cruel rake,

The while the nation's conscience slept;
    Nor did it once awake

Until secession's mighty gun
    At Bull Run so did pelt her
That she, alarmed, compelled, did run
    To Washington for shelter.

'Twas then the thought within her mind
    Occurred to free the slave,
If, by this action, she could find
    A mode her name to save.

Thus, now, you see, the orphan's free,
    So far as slavery's counted,
Yet he is burned, and hanged to tree,
    And chased by fiends well-mounted,

Accused of crime, though innocent,
    He's tortured with strange pleasure:
The wailings of his soul are lent
    To swell her song's blank measure.

Since he was freed he has progressed
    And all the world astounded,
For ne'er have other men possessed
    Such intellect unbounded.

Though hearts of stone and calumny
    Will persecute and murder,

He bears his cross to Calvary,
  Nor falls beneath his burden.

In '98 he volunteered
  To fight for human cause
In foreign land, yet, while he steered
  His son or brother was

Strung up to tree, or stake, or post
  And tortured, cut and burned
And sold by pieces to a host
  Of dastard hearts which turned

To look upon such awful sights,
  Unequaled on this earth
By cannibals or savage rites,
  With coolness and with mirth.

At El Caney and San Juan
  He faced the poisoned lead
And victory brought from among
  Defeat and heaps of dead.

He lay in trench, in mud and mire,
  Through rain, heat and disease,
Nor ever once expressed desire
  That awful place to leave.

O'er dead Caucasian boys he rushed,
  O'er some crouched down with fears,

While from his wounds his warm blood
gushed
And mingled with their tears

He cut the barbed wire fences down
Which did impede his way
And stormed blockhouses on the crown
Of hills; thus gained the day.

He cried when he was not allowed
To enter in the city
The same day that up hill he plowed,
And thought it a great pity

That he might not pursue the foe
Into his place of refuge
And strike at once the final blow,
Thus end the war's grim deluge.

He also garrisoned the land
His bravery had conquered
And made a record which will stand
Among the world's most honored.

And now, that war is waxing hot
In far off Philippines,
And boys of lighter hue do not
Equal their task, it seems,

There's been some talk of sending there
To bring things to a close,

This orphan child of curly hair,
  Broad mouth and flattened nose.

In southern part of this "free" land
  He's not allowed to vote:
They've tied our Constitution's hand
  So that he might be smote.

If he, perchance, commit a crime,
  He's hanged 'thout court proceedings;
His guiltless kin, too, at the time
  Are killed, despite their pleadings.

He's guiltless oft of crime alleged,
  (Which often has been proven,)
But fiends their wealth and life have pledged
  To stagnate law's just movement.

Will someone lend a helping hand,
  Or sympathizing heart,
Or honor pledge and life to stand
  For right on this child's part ?

O, human beings of this earth,
  Arouse your dormant sense
Of right, give merit its true worth
  And claim your recompense!

*Sept., 1899.*

# CONTENT.

Toiling, toiling all day long
  With his will and might,
Humming tune, or whistling song
  From the morn till night:

Ever happy at his work,
  Ever gay and free,
Never does he duty shirk,
  But content is he.

Cheerful is his little home,
  Though of meagre size,
Ne'er he cares from it to roam,
  There his treasure lies,

There his heart's delight is found,
  There his joy and pride,
With his children playing 'round,
  Sweet wife by his side.

Early does he rise at morn,
  To his work he goes
His day's duty to perform
  Without pain or woes.

Fully well is he aware
  Of his family's needs,
Amply does he store prepare,
  And always succeeds.

Thus, the happy father lives
    For his children's sake;
Thus, to them example gives
    Of which they partake.
*Sept., 1899.*

## CAUTION.

The voice speaks often words which are not
    uttered:
The face oft portrays feelings not intended:
The smile expresses things which would be
    smothered:
The mind revives some scenes which are long
    ended:

So measure well the word before 'tis spoken
    And study thoroughly before you've written,
For careless words oft cause hearts to be broken,
    And writing, misconstrued, great hopes has
    smitten.

Learn to control at all times your emotion;
    Don't laugh at others' accidents or errors;
Don't execute your every whim or notion,
    Nor do things which will cause you future
    terrors.

73

Consideration should be first in all things,—
　The execution is subsequent matter,—
For hastiness oft trouble brings that's galling
　And sadness o'er the world promotes and
　　scatters.

Nothing is known until 'tis well experienced:
　No man's so wise that he cannot be wiser:
Judge not a person only by appearance:
　Call no man fool, he may be your adviser.
*Sept., 1899.*

## ONE YEAR AGO.

Just one year ago we broke camp
　In the distant Cuban plain
And began our joyful home tramp
　On the transport and the train.

But, though far from lonely birth land,
　I was happy and content;
I was filled with joy and mirth and
　Happiness where'er I went.

In the lonely life of camping,
　In the mountains wild and drear,

74

Or when through the country tramping,
  Strove I to be of good cheer;

For I loved to ramble often
  Through sweet nature's gorgeous realms:
She has power to soothe and soften
  That which naught else overwhelms.

By the lonely brook and river,
  Laughing in their solitude,
Where the leaves in soft breeze quivered
  And all seemed with life imbued,

Where the birds were gaily chirping,
  Where the fish in deep pools played
And the timid deer were lurking,
  Where the bees their honey made,

In her solemnness of silence
  Nature was at home to me.
In the calmness of that island
  I did live contentedly.

I was wont to sit in quiet,
  Or to roam in loneliness
Through the country wrecked by riot,—
  But which now by peace is blessed,—

Studying language, people, action,
  Or the vegetation there,

Gazing with much satisfaction
  On the products, rich and rare.

Plodding o'er the rugged highlands,
  Through the marshy lands below,
I would pass away the whiles and
  Watch the minutes come and go.

I would sit sometimes for hours
  Basking in the sun's warm rays
While a stream 'neath shady bowers
  Sang to me its favorite lays.

I partook in games athletic
  Which were held among the boys.
I beheld scenes so pathetic
  That they saddened all my joys.

While disease and death were raging
  In the towns and camps around,
While their friends were busy placing
  The deceased beneath the ground,

I was well kept and protected
  By some power of the Unknown,
Which also my way directed
  As I through the wilds did roam:

So I lived in sweet communion
  With the worlds of blue and green

By horizon linked in union,
        In that heaven land of dream.
*March 9, 1900.*


## STRUGGLE WITH TEMPTATION.

What is this haze which now I feel,
Which stealthily begins to steal
About me?   'Tis some magic power
Which comes at this belated hour
To wind me in its grasp.   'Tis strange
This feeling should my mind derange
And cause me such alarm, for I
Have ne'er, in all these years passed by,
Encountered such an influx of
Marauding thought, so hard to solve
As this which now has come to pass.
Methinks awhile some stupor has
O'ershadowed me, and bound my brain
And dimmed my eyes, so that in vain
May I attempt to delve into
The fath'mless depths which now accrue.

It matters not, it seems, how much
Effort I bring to bear to touch
The key-note of this instrument;

The selfsame mystery in extent
Enshrouds its impregnable fort.
Defiance even seems to court
Its presence when from wary tent
Of Indignation he is sent
To battle with this monster, turn
A traitor and betray the urn
Which nourished, kept and cherished him,
Thus cause his guardian much chagrin.

My wits seem somewhat baffled by
The presence of this mighty spy.
I scarce can get my thoughts composed
To right myself.   I'm half disposed
To cease this struggle and allow
Full sway to the usurper, bow
Submissive at its feet, betake
Myself within the walls of fate
And there remain for aye, or till
Such time that I may pass at will
Without this dazed compulsion, free
To think and act contentedly.

*May, 1900.*


## A TALE OF HEARTS.

One night while walking 'long the street,
Returning from the choir,

A young man was involved in thought
  Which burned as though 'twere fire;

For he had seen a girl in church,
  Whom he had known before,
Whose pleading eyes and saddened face
  Seemed deeply to implore

His acquiescence to escort
  Her home at close of church.
He had denied her the request
  And, thinking she might search

The crowd for him, had gone out at
  A side door close to me
And waited till he saw her leave;
  Yet did it not with glee.

'Twas sad: the girl loved him, and said
  He was her heart's desire:
That's why his mind was so involved
  With thought which burned like fire.

He did not wish to mistreat her,
  But he did not love her:
To cherish her fond hopes, then blight
  Them, he did not prefer.

So he was meditating as
  To what course he should strike

When, looking just ahead of him,
 He saw three hearts alike.

At first he thought to crush them all
 And leave them to their fate,
Then quickly thought that he would spare
 Them,—but it was too late:

The blow was struck; one frail heart broke
 And severed into parts:—
I know not what became of it—
 But those were candy hearts.
*June, 1902.*


## A BLIGHTED LIFE.

In the southland of this country
 Lived a happy, wedded pair:
Each content was with the other,
 And their hearts knew no despair.

They were of Caucasian lineage,
 Or, at least, 'twas thought they were,
And no one had e'er disputed
 This, their claim, I may aver.

She was fair, of modest beauty,
 Soft her hair of light brown hue:

He was darker of complexion
  And his hair was darker, too.

So they lived together, happy,
  Never questioning their birth;
Lived in love and adoration
  Close as nature lives to earth.

But ere long they both grew restless
  And they left the balmy South,
Moved to that great northern city
  At the Hudson river's mouth.

They were soon seen out in public
  And occasioned much comment.
Said the gossips; "He is colored."
  This was said where'er they went.

Thus continued they their meddling
  With this couple's happiness:
Thus their prejudice they vented,
  These two young hearts to depress.

Then they said to *her;* "He's colored:
  Has Negro blood in his vein."
Thus tormented they the young bride
  Till her heart relaxed in pain;

Till her soul cried out within her:
  "Is it true;—and if it be,

81

Can I not still live and love him?
  Can he not still live for me?"

"Can we not remain together?
  I do not question his kin.
It may be true,—yet, I love him.—
  Can there be a diff'rence, then?"

Thus she wailed and strove with reason.—
  Would she overcome the blow?
Could she not raise an embankment
  That would dam their gossip's flow?

No—alas! her heart was failing.
  They would separate, she thought:
So decided she and acted;
  Left him, and a fairer sought.

But her soul was not contented:
  She could love no one but him,
For her life to his was mated.
  God had made their souls a twin.

Thus some people of this country,
  Who, by chance, are very light,
Tear asunder the Almighty's
  Work and claim that they are right.

Is there not some power of conscience
  That will cleanse their hearts and souls?

Are there no Caucasian Christians
　　'Tween these two terrestrial poles?
*July, 1903.*


# A STUDENT'S CHRISTMAS PARTING.

[Published in the Exonian, Phillips Exeter Academy.]

Farewell, ye halls of red and gray!
Nay; Au revoir! I'd rather say!
Ye campus grounds now bleak and drear!
Ye buildings to my heart made dear!
Ye chapel walls, your songs bestir!
I leave you now, old Exeter.

Ye books and pen I lay aside
To rest you, calm and unespied.
I go to greet the coming year,
To welcome him with mirth and cheer.
Vacation time is near at hand
When all is joy throughout our land.

Ere long again I'll greet you all,
And from your slumber calm I'll call.
I'll bring with me a newer strain
To fill your corridors again.

83

I'll bring with me a heart so free
'Twill fill your stolid walls with glee.

The folk at home are waiting now;
Already is the holly bough
Made into wreath of red and green
To grace the beauty of the scene.
Again, ye hall and corridor,
I turn to bid you, Au revoir!
*Dec.,1903.*


## ADVICE TO A FRIEND.

You say that virtue is its own
Reward: I'm sure that's widely known,
Yet, while I wish not to pursuade
You to refuse the request made,

I think that our reward is found
When satisfaction does abound
In feeling that our work is not
Ungratefully scorned or forgot.

For no reward can truly be
Unless received with feeling free,
Unless 'tis given from the heart,
Unless 'tis made of life a part.

We often may feel that we should
Our talents lend for doing good;
We also oft may later find
That the return is quite unkind.

So I should say, be sure that you
Consider well the step in view,
Yet do not fail to full regard
That virtue is its own reward.

*Feb., 1904.*


# THE MINOR CHORD OF LIFE.

[Published in the Exeter News-Letter.]

Is there not a hand of power
   That can stay the wheel of fate?
Is there not a soothing hour
   For sad hearts that mourn and wait?

Can no recompense their longings
   Find while wand'ring through this life?
Must no sunlight pierce their mornings
   With its many-pointed knife?

Must they wander through existence
   With their heavy burdens bent?

Must no heart lend them assistance?
   Must no hope to them be lent?

Fain would some assistance offer,
   But it satisfies them not;
Others fain would comfort proffer,
   But their comfort comforts not.

Some would gladly shelter give them,
   But the storms still rage within;
Others with bright hopes would cheer them,
   But to them all hopes are dim.

These sad hearts possess a longing
   Which no earthly power can soothe;
There's a strain to them belonging
   Which the hardest heart would move.

Yet, these souls are meek, forgiving,
   Patient, though time nothing brings.—
Life would not be worth the living
   If no sorrow tuned its strings.

*April, 1904.*


## FROM THE STAGE OF LIFE.

Once there was a happy youth
   With heart as light and free

And gleeful as a lamb at play,
  As merry as could be.

No morning sun e'er rose on him
  That did not see him smile;
No evening twilight sank to rest
  And left him sad the while.

No bird at daybreak sweeter sang
  Than did his whistling note;
No youth nor maiden was more kind,
  Nor any kinder spoke.

But now those days have long since gone,—
  They can return no more,—
And he, once innocent and blithe,
  Is changed e'en to the core.—

Oh, cruel fate that wrought the deed
  That turned his heart to stone,
That stole away his innocence,
  And left his soul alone,

Thou might'st have done a kinder thing
  And yet deserved thy name!
But no: thou wouldst not kinder be
  And save a life from shame.—

One day he met a pretty maid,
  Of rather modest mien,

Whose love for him he read as soon
  As he her face had seen.

He liked her, too, and often was
  In company with her,
And as the days and weeks passed by
  Much more attached they were.

But yet he hardly loved the girl,
  Though she loved him, she said;
So he had dared think—to himself—
  That some day they would wed.

But then the tempter came to her
  And she, poor suffering girl,
Could not resist, but yielded up
  Her honor, her life's pearl.

Her face, from then, was different
  Than he had seen before;
She could not look straight in his eyes;
  She trembled more and more.

He asked her what the matter was:
  She said 'twas nothing much;
But, since he had observed, he could
  Not be content with such.

So he began to question her,
  And she, 'mid tears and pain,

Confessed and begged that he forgive
   And take her back again.—

Oh, cruel dart that pierced his breast
   And left thy flint head where
A heart did once in pleasure throb,
   Thou'st robbed his bosom's lair. —

He could not think the same of her;
   He cherished naught but scorn;
He chided her with fiendish glee:
   She was downcast, forlorn.

"False woman, why didst thou not think
   Of all this shame and woe,"
Said he, " ere yielding up thy name
   And maidenhood?   Now go!"

"And never let me see thy face
   Again here on this earth
While life shall last and I have breath,
   While honor has its worth."

"Thou saidst to me that thou didst love
   Me, but hast proved a lie,
And now hast impudence to ask
   That I forgive.   Could I

Forgive a thousand times thy wrong,
   I never should forget

Thy bland, deceitful countenance,
　　Thy promise false.—And yet,

Was it thy fault that thou didst yield
　　And barter thy good name
To one of such ignoble birth
　　For ignominious shame?"—

"Ah yes; too well thou knew his tale
　　Of life, his character;
Too well thou knew what he had been;
　　Full well knew who thou were."

"Hadst thou not known his vile repute,
　　Nor designed his intent,
Hadst not been warned nor cautioned 'gainst
　　The way in which thou went,

There might, perchance, be some excuse
　　For this mishap of thine :
Thou hast gone headlong into it;
　　Thou must now wail and pine."

"Thy future life shall be despair,
　　Thy past one deep regret;
Thy lonely hours shall be in shame;
　　Nor shalt thou e'er forget

The purity which once was thine,
　　The pleasure of those days

When thou wert clothed in virtuous robe,
  When thou wert chaste in ways."

"The phantom of thy purer life
  Shall haunt thee in thy sleep;
The terror of thy faded bloom
  Shall pierce thy day dreams deep."

"Thy bare existence until death
  Shall be as Hades dark;
Thy reddened glare of tainted love
  Shall glow a mere, small spark."

"The liking which I had for thee
  Is gone fore'er; has flown
Away to find a worthier soul—
  And left me sad, alone."

"But yet, Fate hath not baffled me;
  I have a weapon still.
Though one has proven false to me,
  I cannot and I will

Not think that womankind is false,
  That none is good and pure,
For I've a mother, sisters too,
  Whom I'd profane, I'm sure,

Were I to countenance such thought.
  Such vile indecency

Is for some baser animal
    Than I could ever be."

His faith, though shattered, was not lost;
    He would not all condemn
Because this one had done a wrong:
    Such thought was base to him.
*July, 1904.*

## PRESENTATION POEM.

[Written for my sister Allene.]

Dear Friend, my teacher for the bygone term,
    Accept this token of my love for thee,
For from thee many lessons did I learn
    And much of thy blithe, kindly nature see.

Thy kindness unto me and loving care
    While through the streets of knowledge I
    did roam,
Thy willingness, benevolent and fair,
    To teach and tell me things which thou
    hast known,

Which always do portray themselves so well
    In thy expressive countenance, thy smile,

And which to all beholding do foretell
  Thy kind intentions towards  them  all  the
    while

To make them happy, by thy blithesome face,
  Thy beauteous, characteristic grace,
Time ne'er shall from my memory erase,
  Though  many  years  be  swallowed  into
    space.

This simple token, though of little worth,
  And of the things which  transpire  here  on
    earth,
Expressive is of feeling which was born
  Out of kind treatment, which no heart  can
    scorn.
*June, 1899.*


## HALLOWE'EN.

[To a Friend.]

Last night was Hallowe'en, you know;
  The cowbells rang, the horns did blow,
The goblins stalked o'er stones and planks
  And small boys played their annual pranks.

The women dressed in men's attire;
  The small girl, too, quenched her desire

93

To get into her brother's pants:
  The hollow pumpkin had its chance.

The sidewalks creaked, the street cars balked,
  The sign boards moved, the lamp posts
    mocked,
The wagons went to roof resorts
  And front gates climbed poles of all sorts.

The Indians at tobacco stores
  Went on the warpath by the scores.
The ticktacks played on window panes
  And stuffed men mounted weather vanes.

The larger boys played other tricks;
  They tied dogs' tails to large-sized bricks:
Pinned placards on policemen's coats
  And set fire to the tails of goats.

They masked themselves as spooks and
    ghosts
  And stood behind trees and big posts;
They set logs 'gainst some folk's front doors,
  Then knocked and ran away, of course.

They put torpedoes on the rails
  For streetcars, and painted cats' tails;
And many more such things as these
  They did, which you may name with ease;

For, if you were not once a boy,
    I'm rather sure you did enjoy,
At some time, hearing stories told
    Of how the boys did do of old.

But boys must have their fun and play,
    Although they often have to pay
Quite dearly for their tricks and sport,
    Which sometimes wind up in a court.

Yet, boys can play their pranks and jokes
    On numerous good-natured folks
Who think that boys must have their fun,
    E'en though they sometimes have to run.

So Hallowe'en may come and go,
    And cranky folk may often show
Their temper, but the boys don't care;
    For what's a boy who will not dare?
*Nov., 1904.*


## AS WE SHOULD BE.

We should be as kind and cheerful
    As we can here on this earth;
For in Heav'n we may be judged by
    What our work in life is worth.

Life may not always be pleasant,
    We may oft feel grieved and sad,
But we should not think that others
    Have not sadness as we had.

Some are rich, enjoying pleasures
    Of this world with careless ease;
Some are poor and laden with much
    Sorrow, deeper than the seas;

Yet we all should be contented,
    Whether rich, poor, sad, or gay,
For this life is what we make it.—
    There's some sunshine every day.
*Oct., 1905.*


## A VALUED LESSON.

[Thought upon leaving Exeter.]

I sat beneath a stately elm,
    While Autumn round me threw her cloak,
As though she would my mind o'erwhelm
    With thoughts of other lands and folk.

And as she fanned my solemn brow
    With a refreshing, cooling breeze,
I fell to thinking of the now
    And of the then that is to be:

96

That I am now a student poor
    In knowledge of this universe,
With many hardships to endure
    Ere I may ope that valued purse.

And as I sat reflecting 'lone,
    A little bee came flying near
In search of honey for his cone
    To feed him through the winter drear.

He lighted on a tiny flower,
    Which swayed and bent beneath his
        weight,
But finding not sufficient dower,
    He flew away and left it straight.

But there his efforts did not end,
    He tried another, and one more,
And yet again he tried to rend
    Some from another for his store.

And as I turned unto my strain
    Of thinking, I bethought me so:
If now I fail, I'll try again;
    I shall succeed some time, I know.

And in the then that is to come
    I'll look back o'er the trodden hill
And view what persistence has done.—
    There's no success without some will.
*Sept., 1905.*

97

# A WESTERN REVERIE.

### (Song—To my sisters.)

[Written on a U. P. Train in Wyoming.]

When the sun sets o'er the hills in the desolate,
  wild west
  And its crimson, golden light fades into blue,
And the dusky drab of eve steals up o'er their
  rugged crest,
  Then it is, my dearest hearts, I think of you.
When the far-off curling smoke from a camp-
  fire on the plain
  Wends its heav'nward way far up into the sky,
And the dim and reddened glare of the disap-
  pearing flame
  Fades from sight, 'tis then I wish that you
  were nigh.

When the sky is gold and blue
  I am thinking still of you,
As the setting sun displays his latest ray;
  And when night steals o'er the plain
Thoughts of you arise again,
  And my heart can find no rest, so far away.

Night then draws her starry veil o'er her dark-
  ened, blushing face
  And reflects the gentle memories of day,

98

And the moon peeps o'er the hill from her cozy
    hiding place
    And pours out her soul in light across my
       way.
Then, as constellations rise slowly on their up-
    ward climb,
    And the north star, too, lends me her silver
       gleam,
Phantom visions of you cross the horizon of my
    mind,
    And I slumber through the beauty of the
       dream.
*Aug., 1905.*


## VALE DICO.

Dear Exeter, I fare thee well !
    Fore'er I leave thy hallowed halls !
What I've endured, no one can tell,
    Save my sad heart locked in its walls.

This heart was not so sad always,
    It had a blithesome, happy strain ;
But now, alas ! it's changed its lays
    To doleful lines, more doleful pain.

And not because I hate thee do
    I take my leave of thee for aye,
But 'tis because I love thee true
    And fear to hurt thee if I stay.

For I am human, with a right
    Of life, with feelings, and a soul,
And 'gainst race prejudice I'll fight
    As long as I can weapons hold.

Thy sons to me, except a few
    Have been as brothers and as men ;
Have been as fathers to me through
    Adversities that proved them friends.

But some there were as opposite
    To them as poison is to sweets ;
Whose souls were vile and ill befit
    To mingle 'mong thy walls and streets.

I noted well the hearty cheer
    And welcome from these greater souls:
I noted, too, with careful ear,
    The silence of those narrow moles.

I noted well the hearty grip,
    The pleasant mien, the strong, firm voice,
I noted, too, that limpid slip
    Which names the knave of narrow choice.

If thou couldst speak, I feel well sure
　　That thou wouldst shame those baser hearts,
That thou wouldst shun them as impure
　　And bid them to their 'customed parts.

For thy gate, Phillips did decree,
　" Shall ever open be to youth
From every quarter, equally,"
　　Whose principles are right and truth.

Now, as I go, I bid thee feel
　　With all my heart I say, Adieu !
Some other hall shall train my zeal
　　My future destiny to woo.
*Oct., 1905*.


## ON THE DEATH OF DUNBAR.

[To his Mother]

Is Dunbar gone, forever and for aye ?
　　No, he is not ! his soul has never died ;
His spirit form is with us through our day ;
　　Nor in our night does it desert our side.

Though sweet " Li'l' Gal " may weep, " Ma-
　　lindy " mourn,
　" The Party " veil its face with solemn crepe

In sorrow for him of whom they were born ;
  And though we, too, may weep at his sad
    fate ;

Yet one consoling thought remains to cheer
  Us in this hour of lamentation deep :
His soul yet lives, is with us year by year.
  He is not dead, for in our midst he sleeps

Enfolded 'tween the covers of his books.
  The old tree, torn with bullets, by the road
Still moans the story of its deadened looks ;
  The " Ole Mule," with his lazy human load,

Still plods along his weary homeward way ;
  " Malindy Sings " as sweetly to our mind ;
The " Uncalled " hovers round us as to sway
  Our lives with " Lyrics," poetry and rhyme.

We need but to unfold his clothbound bier,
  To take him from his grave upon our shelves
And lend his inmost soul our closest ear,
  And Dunbar lives, and speaks, e'en as our-
    selves.

A life we mourn which late we oft extolled ;
  A work unfinished, yet complete, we read,

Like his, our lives, our talents will unfold
  And bloom with beauty, if our hearts we
    heed.
*Feb., 1906.*


## WRITTEN AT THE REQUEST OF A SKEPTIC.

To-day the brllliant sunbeam hangs
  O'er all our joys, our cares,
Removing all of sorrow's pangs,
  Depicting all its snares.

'Tis nature's cloak of soothing dreams
  She throws about our life,
Admitting naught of sorrow's beams
  To mar our upward strife.
*May, 1906.*


## WRITTEN IN AN ALBUM.
### [To L. F. C.]
When you find yourself in sorrow,
  Weighted down by care and strife,
Raise the curtain of the morrow
  And behold a brighter life.
*May, 1906.*

# FIDELITY.

Sweetheart, for love of you, I'd give
   Up all the pleasures of this life,
And be content fore'er to live
   And love you, though through endless strife.

I'd give up all the joys of earth
   For love of you, my dearest heart ;
I'd forfeit e'en my right of birth,
   Than that your love from me should part.

The fiercest storms of life I'd brave
   If but your love were the reward.
I'd cross the sea of pain's dread wave,
   Nor would I one complaint record,

Nor say, nor feel one faint regret,
   If 'twere for love of you I sailed;
I'd suffer untold grief, and yet,
   No mortal ear should know I wailed.

I'd sever all the earthly ties
   That bind me to a living soul
And journey upward to the skies,
   If I but thought your love the goal.

I'd suffer all that cruel word
   And unkind act could e'er inflict

Upon my heart, if I but heard,
  One pledge of favor from your lip.

I'd suffer death a thousandfold
  For one sweet kiss from you, my dear,
If I your love might have and hold,
  For death were naught if love were here.
*Nov., 1905.*


## SATAN'S DREAM.

[Scene based upon L. Christine Jensen's "Life."]

Ah! Dead! What! Dead! My favorite prince!
Thou, whom I sent out not long since
To check those Christians on their way
To Paradise!—I'll curse the day
That saw this deed!—Ah! Yes 'tis true!
But look they well; this day they'll rue.
Poor prince, brave prince, thy royal blood
Shall be avenged:   I'll cause a flood
Of Christian souls to fall, for this,
Down into my deep, dark abyss.
Ye habitants of my abode,
Come, rally, dance, mine anger goad,
And register this vow:   I swear
By thunderbolt and lightning's glare
That I'll avenge my prince's death,

That I will draw no restful breath
Until I've brought their haughty souls
And cast them on my bed of coals.

But hark!   Methinks I hear a voice!
Ah, yes!   'Tis they!—Fools make your choice;
This day shall be the last you'll see,
For ere the morrow ye shall be
Locked in my deepest, darkest cell.
I know my elves will treat you well:
For bread they'll give you burning coals;
For water, teeming, seething bowls
Of hottest blazes of my realm;
When tired, your souls they'll overwhelm
With tortures vilest e'er conceived.
Then Faith and Hope and Love must leave;
They cannot live within my gate,
For with me dwell Despair and Hate.

Ha! Ha!   Proud Faith, thou'st battled well;
Before thy sword my captain fell;
But thou dost battle now his peer
Who causeth earth to quake with fear,
Who holdeth lightning at command
And sendeth thunder through the land,
Who visiteth the earth with plagues
Until the haughty Christian begs

For mercy.    So, proud Faith, look sharp:
I'll yet destroy thy magic art.

I'll show thee that the Tempter's power
Can overcome thee, make thee cower:
I'll teach thee that revenge is sweet,
While thou dost grovel at my feet.
Then I, Satan, who once did quail
Before thy gaze, shall mock thy wail:
I, who the while was terrified
By thy bright glare, shall hail with pride
The victory: and I shall wreak
My vengeance on both strong and weak:
I'll overrun the land with wrong
And scatter discord 'mongst thy throng
Of idle followers.    Then I
Shall rule supreme o'er earth and sky:
So, Faith, and Hope, and Love, take care—
Ha! Ha! Ha! Ha! Ha! Ha!—Beware!
*Jan., 1906.*


## TO THE ORGAN.

[Written in Payson Church, Easthampton, Mass.]

O, mass of tone immaculate,
Of harmony most intricate,

107

So beautiful, so consecrate,
  I love to listen to thy song
As through my melancholy soul
  It pours its torrents sweet and long.
I love to listen to thy swell,
For thou dost deep emotions tell.
  My inmost soul is moved and thrilled
With joy, with sorrow, sweetness, hope,
  My life with harmony is filled,
When thy great volume bursts the air,
Or soft, steals on me unaware;
  The world with lyric beauty teems;
My swift imagination sails
  Through seas of melody, and dreams.
A soul thou hast inborn, innate;
And yet, thou art inanimate,
  Thou mass of tone immaculate.
*Oct., 1906.*


## TO A ROSE AT WILLISTON.

[The rose which grows behind South Hall.]

Pretty, ruby, half-blown rose,
  Grown upon our campus green,
Tell me, have you any woes?
  Are you happy as you seem?

Tell me, ere your beauty fade,
  Ere your fragrant odor wane
'Neath this dormitory's shade,
  Have you ever known a pain?

Oft I've passed behind this hall
  To my lessons, to the well,
And you, crouched beneath the wall,
  Seemed to have some tale to tell.

Tell me why your cheeks are red;
  Are you blushing, dainty flower?
Why sometimes you droop your head;
  Is't your melancholy hour?

Have you heard the leaves are dying?
  Have you seen them turn and fall?
Have the autumn breezes, sighing,
  Whispered to you nature's call?

Come, my beauty, tell me, pray,
  Should I pluck you in your bloom
Would you live for me one day,
  Just to brighten up my room?

'Twere a pity I should take
  You, sweet, red rose, from your thorn,
Yet, the chill winds make you quake
  And ere long you will be gone:

Gone into that great unknown,
  Where the beautiful of earth
Springs up and matures, full blown,
  In a realm of song and mirth.

So I'll pluck you, rosebud shy,
  From your thorn-bush, chill and cold,
That your fragrance, as you die,
  May be breathed into my soul.

Then I'll press and keep you, rose,
  Though your ruby hue be gone,
To remind me, as time goes,
  Of my life at Williston.
*Oct., 1906.*


## THE DEATH OF THE LEAVES.

[Published in the Willistonian, Williston Seminary.]

Green the grass is on the campus,
  But the leaves are turning brown
As the melancholy autumn
  Spreads the hoar frost o'er the ground.

Quivering, the leaves are waiting
  For the call from earth's dark mold,

For she needs them to protect her
  From the winter's ice and cold.

When they hear her call, they scamper
  From their lofty summer home
Back to mother earth, who gave them,
  Whence they never more may roam.

Silently they do their bidding;
  Carefully their carpet weave,
So that when their work is finished,
  No uncovered spot they leave.

Closely to her breast they hover,
  That her life-blood be not chilled,
Till the sun returns in springtime,
  When their mission is fulfilled.

But the breezes miss their presence,
  Dancing gaily in their wake,
So, in sorrow, sighing, moaning,
  They bewail their playmates' fate.

Colder grow their hearts from sighing;
  Louder grow their moans and wails,
Till their moist tears turn to snowflakes,
  Covering o'er the new made graves.

And the barren trees, too, weeping,
  Lash the chill winds with their limbs

Till to icicles their tears are
   Frozen by the angry winds.

Then the wood-birds leave the forest,
   For they find no pleasure there
Since the little leaves have fallen
   And the trees are in despair.

   So we should employ our lifetime
   That our friends may moan and grieve
When we leave this world, as do the
Trees and winds the little leaves.
*Oct., 1906.*

## WRITTEN ON A CHRISTMAS GIFT.

[To M. E. G.]

When you're lonely or in sorrow,
   Wipe away your burning tears
With this token of a friendship
   Which, yet short, may last through years:

And when you have reached the highest
   Step upon the stair of fame,
Turn and wave to me this kerchief;
   I'll be somewhere in the train.
*Dec., 1905.*

# MY SISTERS

Would you like to know who occupy the best
    place in my heart ?
  It's a secret but I'll tell you if you'll promise
    not to tell,
For I think they're just the sweetest girls, and
    Oh ! they are so smart
That I love them very dearly—Oh, you've
    guessed it, have you ?   Well,
Now I don't care if you do know, for they're all
    the world to me,
And I like to have you know it.—They're my
    sisters; don't you see ?
Yes, my sisters are the dearest girls that I have
    ever met:
I loved them before I knew it, and my love I
    don't regret.
I was bashful when I found it out, and wouldn't
    say I did,
But I'm not afraid to own it now, for I am not
    a "kid."
*1907.*

# THE DAY OF REST.

The day of rest is soon to come
When we'll fly to our eternal home
Where we shall dwell in peace and rest
Among the myriads of the blest
Who have been called from earthly cares,
From toils and trials and despairs
To that dear land where peace doth reign,
Where sorrow can no foothold gain.

And when we reach that paradise
And stand before our Lord and Christ,
We'll praise His name, for he hath giv'n
To us a peaceful home in heav'n.
We there shall meet our loved of yore,
Who now are waiting at the door.
Within that home we'll dwell alway,
Through time and everlasting day.

O Lord, we thank Thee for that home,
Where we can rest, no more to roam,
Where everlasting light doth 'bide
And never doth its glory hide.
There in that peaceful bliss we'll live,
Wrapt in the robe which Thou dost give
To those who will accept Thy love
And sing Thy praises as above.
*1897.*

# ON THE GIFT OF A WHISKBROOM.

[To R. C. R., Jr.]

When you have swept on wings of fame
  Far past these souls more common sired,
Pray, brush the dead dust from your name,
  That I may view and be inspired.
*Dec., 1905.*


# ON THE GIFT OF A THERMOMETER

[To A. L. C.]

When you have soared thorough dizzy air
  And cut your name on fame's high cliff,
Please take the temperature there
  And drop it to me as a gift.
*Dec., 1905.*


# ON A CLOTHES BRUSH.

As you may brush your clothes at times,
So that no grain of dust remain
        To mar their good aspect,
I ask one favor through these lines;
That you will keep the giver's name
        Free from dust of neglect.
*Dec., 1905.*

115

# THE HEARTS OF AMERICA.

[To a Friend.]

The heart of the South, my little girl,
    Is as hard and rigid as stone;
It tortures to death with knife and flame
    Those of flesh and blood of its own.

The heart of the North, my little maid,
    Is as ice, so frigid, so cold;
It listens and looks, but answers not
    To the wails of colored folk's souls.

The heart of the South, my little child,
    Is as black as midnight with crime;
Nor can it erase those murd'rous stains
    Through the endless ages of time,

The heart of the North, my wond'ring babe,
    Is devoid of feeling as steel;
It enforces not our country's laws,
    Although millions of us appeal.

The heart of the Negro, little dear,
    Which was once so tender and kind,
Is bitter against both South and North,
    Since in neither justice it finds.

But Liberty's heart, my little one,
    May be sleeping, but is not dead;

116

And when it awakes, as soon it must,
    There may be some rivers of red.

The heart of the man oppressed and wronged
    Yearns for vengeance, justice and right,
And once it begins its angry course
    It increases much fold in might.

The Negro, who would not dare to stand
    Fighting bravely for life and home,
Is worth but to live a traitor's life;
    But to die unclaimed by his own.
*Dec., 1906.*


## TO A BUNCH OF CARNATIONS.

### (Dedicated to the Donors.)

[Published in the Enterprise, Easthampton.]

I wonder if you, flowers, know
    The happiness you bring to me.
I wonder if you have a soul,
    And feel my gratitude and glee.

I wonder if your pretty smile
    And pleasant face, your graceful form
Were stolen from your donors while
    They placed their dainty card hereon.

I wonder if you felt the thrill
   Of joy you gave my lonely heart:
I wonder if your petals still
   Will live, when their sweet odors part

'Tis sad to think that you must die
   And all your beauty fade away,
Not even in a grave to lie
   And moulder till some brighter day.

But yours a mission is of love,
   Of good, of happiness, of faith:
Sent by the power from above,
   You cheer the great, nor scorn the waif.

'Tis sad to think you have no voice,
   That you might tell your heart's intent:
'Tis sad to know you have no choice
   To leave me e'en your fragrant scent.

I wish I had the power to give
   You back unto your root and vine:
I wish you might forever live
   To cheer the lonely souls that pine:

But otherwise it has been willed,
   And you, departing, leave the race,
Yet, leave our lives with treasure filled
   Because your life was love and grace.
*March, 1907.*

# TO A FRIEND.

A sweet little soul have you, my dear,
A heart that is true, in love sincere,
A manner so kind, a grace so true
That hardly could one help loving you.

Nor this do I say without intent;
'Tis not for mere praise nor flatt'ry meant;
It is my belief, from what I've seen
And studied of you through music's screen.

As one cannot know his real worth
While making abode here on this earth,
So you cannot see, perhaps, these traits
Which surely your being permeate.

And I think it not amiss to tell
You of your good traits I see so well,
For, knowing what good we do possess
May urge us yet more to righteousness.

Quite much have I traveled o'er these lands,
Heard many a voice, grasped many hands,
Seen many a face, and read each heart;—
Experience has lent me her art.

So, bringing this knowledge, dearly gained,
To bear on your case, I feel sustained

In saying, as you have read above,
That yours is a worthy soul to love.

With hatred of race this land throughout,
On perjury founded by the South,
'Tis pleasant, and worthy of much praise
To find souls like yours to light the ways.

The soul has no color but of eyes,
Possesses no malice, no disguise;
The soul knows no creed but love and faith;
It knows only man; it knows no race.

That such is the soul within your breast;
Your actions and deeds do full attest.
And to such a soul alone is given
That happiness which we call our heaven.
*Feb., 1907.*


## THE BURIAL OF THE PAST.

Let this the funeral of our difference be;
Let each the other tell the soul's desire;
Let each disdain the other's faults to see,
And let our hearts be kindled with that fire
That melts two dispositions into one
And then withdraws therefrom its greater heat

And leaves the molten mass, its mission done,
With warmth of love in unity complete.
But let us not forget that faults are ours,
Nor be unmindful of their secret growth,
But ever strive with all our latent powers
The ideal of perfection to approach.
Then as our lives are blended in one strain
And two hearts with the selfsame impulse throb,
With one consoling thought, each mind the
     same,
May we be happy while above the sod.
*Jan., 1907.*

## IN MAY.

[Written for The Enterprise, Easthampton, Mass.]

In May we launch our swift canoe,
    Unbind the sail and hoist her,
And at the same time bid adieu
    To our good friend, the oyster.
*May, 1907.*

# WRITTEN ON A CHRISTMAS CARD.

[To I. H.]

A friendship true is rare indeed,
  So, I would cherish thine,
For friendship springs from sincere hearts,
  From sentiment divine.

*Dec., 1907.*


# A NOVEMBER SABBATH MORN.

[On Belmont Heights, Springfield, Mass.]

Early on one Sunday morning
  Ere the Autumn had grown old,
I arose from peaceful sleep and
  Dressed myself to take a stroll.

Down the crooked streets I wandered
  Till I met a winding road
Following a deep, walled brooklet
  Which, with lazy vigor flowed

Through a pretty, narrow valley,
  Draining all the neighboring hills
By a system of large drain pipes
  And two busy little rills.

122

Following this road, I crossed the
    Stream and bore off to the left,
Climbing up a hill through which a
    Narrow street was being cleft.

Strolling 'cross this meadowed hilltop
    In a brisk refreshing breeze,
I imbibed the breath of morning
    Wafted to me by the trees.

But the leaves and grass were dying,
    Worn out by the summer's toil,
E'en the little breeze was sighing,
    For no warmth was in the soil.

Drowsily the sun came peeping
    O'er the housetops on the height,
Blushing at his late arising,
    Flooding all the heav'n with light.

From the brow of Belmont Heights my
    Vision wandered 'cross the vale
To the far-off, peaceful river,
    Winding down its crooked trail.

Towering from the valley rose the
    Pointed steeples, spires and domes,
As though watching o'er the clusters
    At their feet of quiet homes.

123

Busily the engines glided
  'Long their steel roads 'mong the mills,
Or on bridges o'er the river.
  As a background, tiers of hills

Stretched their rugged, dark-hued ranges
  As a wall on either side,
Stalked with pines, and here a windmill
  Sluggishly its labor plied.

O'er this picture hung a blue haze,
  Frightened by the rising sun
And retreating from his splendor,
  For the day had now begun.

O'er the blue sky, like a snowdrift,
  Spread a thin, white, drifted cloud
Veiling o'er the moon's pale visage,
  Trailing 'round her like a shroud.

Pale, yet bravely and defiant,
  Stood the mistress of the night
Battling with the "great task-master,"
  But unequal in the fight.

All the little stars had hidden
  When at first they saw him rise,
For they knew that he would scold them
  If they stayed out in the skies.

So, in glory, still advancing,
    Came he on that Sabbath morn,
Striking with his rays the church bells
    Till their tongues chimed forth in song.

Long stood I admiring, wond'ring,
    Dreaming o'er the beauteous scene,
Painting it with brush of mem'ry
    On my mind's receptive screen.
*Nov., 1906.*


## TO THE WIND OF THE NIGHT.

Wind of the night, thou silent guardian
    Of the peaceful hours of life,
Bring unto me some missent message
    From some heart o'ercome with strife;

Bring to me some belated message
    From some heart o'erfilled with love;
Whisper to me some long-kept secret
    Of some soul now gone above.

Steed of the air, thou swift conveyor
    Of the seasons of our sphere,
Bear to my heart that youth, that vigor
    Born of happiness and cheer.

Breath of the moon, thou great proclaimer
    Of the power of our God,
Voice of the trees, and yet the murmur
    Of the lowly shrub, the sod,

Breathe to my soul some consolation
    Made to soothe a lonely mind,
Tell to my ear some story brightened
    With the promises of time.

Leave me not here alone to ponder,
    Waft me to some land of dreams
Where I may find a sweet communion,
    For life is not as it seems.
*Nov., 1906.*


## DESOLATION.

How desolate is life for those
Who live within the wall of woes;
Who come into this world of care
With naught but sorrow for their share;
Who pine and long for love, for light,
For riches, learning, or for might;
Who dream by night and toil by day,
Nor aught can find to drive away

This restlessness, this grim desire,
Nor e'en to satisfy it's ire!

The coyote on the western plain
Which hardly sagebrush can sustain,
Which knows no moisture save the dew,
Which boasts no tree to break the view,
Contented with the desert is,
For all that he surveys is his.

The lean gray wolf that haunts the cave,
Whose dreadful howl makes e'en the brave
Man shudder when at first he feels
His shriek which near his blood congeals,
That dogs the herd and picks with care
The fattest bullock for his share,
Desires no different life to lead;
For much he finds to sate his greed.

The rabbit, bounding o'er the sands,
Or nibbling sagebrush as he stands
Or crouches, resting from his play,
Quite satisfied is there to stay;
For there his pleasure he pursues
And there he burrows, broods and woos.

The eagle, sailing through the air,
Or screaming from the high cliffs, bare,
Or swooping down upon some flock,

Or perched upon some lonely rock,
Is happy in his loneliness;
For there securely he may rest.

But he who of this human stock
Is happy with his earthly lot,
Who has no troubles, cares, nor pains,
Who knows no loss, but ever gains,
Exists not in this world of strife,
Except in that ideal life;
That life for which men pine and yearn.
So, as some live their years, they learn
That life is bare and desolate,
That all is ruled by cruel fate,
And though they strive to do, to know,
They're choked by penury and woe.
*Oct. 1906.*


## HE WHO LAUGHED LAST,
## LAUGHED BEST.

A youth there was, of not great education,
Who thought to raise himself above his station;
And so, by constant toil and application
He pulled up some few points in estimation;

And when this he had done
He thought his fame was won.—
A small work he compiled—
And all the people smiled.

But dauntlessly he toiled then all the harder,
For he'd resolved that he would go much farther,
He knew that life was hard for any starter,
And he was not afraid to be a martyr.
So he made up his mind
He'd try a second time;—
And at this paragraph
The people fairly laughed.

But not discouraged by this second failure,
His resolution donned a third regalia
And sallied forth this time as an assailer:
And then began the scoffers to look paler;
For they must now confess
That he had made success.
They saw that they had blundered—
And all the people wondered.
*Nov., 1906.*

## A TALE OF A YOUTH OF BROWN.

Out from the plains of Illinois,
Out from the town of Lincoln's home,
Where the emancipator's tomb
Answers the stare of state house dome,
    Came forth a strippling of a boy.

Brown as a chestnut was his face,
Brown as two beans his soulful eyes,
Curly his hair like waves and black,
Bright was his face as summer skies:
    He was of Afric's sunburnt race.

"Sweet was his whistle as a birds',"
"Courteous his manner as could be,"
Buoyant his spirits as the air,
Light was his heart, so young, so free,
    "Mellow his voice as ever heard."

He was denied his chief desire,
Taken from school, fore'er, perhap,
But he, undaunted by his fate,
Ran away from his mother's lap;
    Left to escape his father's ire.

To the great city came this lad,
As yet unskilled in worldly lore,

Sought out employment for himself.
During his leisure he would pore
    Over some book, some song he had.

    Studied and worked he much by night,
Painted, and sang, and whistled, drew
Pictures and whittled toys from wood,
Did as he thought he ought to do,
    Lived as he knew and loved the right;

    For he had known a mother's care,
Felt of her anguish and her joy,
Heard his grandmother, late a slave,
Reading of David, shepherd boy,
    Guarding his flocks from beast and snare.

    Growing, this youth to manhood came,
But he had not what he loved best,
Clamored his heart to learn, to know,
Nor could he feel content, at rest,
    For he had vowed to rise to fame.

    Finally heard he of a school
Where he might work, and in return
Receive the knowledge which he wished.
Forthwith he went, alas, to learn
    That southern prejudice there ruled.

    Famed was this school throughout the land.
Even from o'er the seas there came

Youth to be educated, trained,
Not only in the paths of fame,
But in base hatred, man for man.

Sad, but resolved, he left its walls,
Went to a more congenial one
Where he might have a right to live;
He found this right at Williston;
Found justice, freedom in her halls;

Found friendly spirit in her town;
Found helping hands and willing hearts
Brightened, his soul poured forth its strains,
Pleasing the townsfolk with his arts
Until they loved this youth of brown.
*Dec., 1906.*


## MEDITATIONS OF A NEGRO'S MIND.  V.

With wailing souls and protests came
Our fathers to this virgin soil,
Deprived of freedom and in chain,
Denied the product of their toil.

Compelled to learn the white man's art,
They learned to love the white man's God,

132

And though not of his race a part,
    They were engrafted to the sod.

For ages they were wronged and robbed
    And on the spoils this nation thrived;
For centuries they prayed and sobbed
    Until their prayers were recognized.

But, though they broke the iron band
    And left us freedom, as 'tis called,
We still are bondsmen in this land,
    By unjust laws and treatment thralled.

But this much longer cannot be,
    For we will protest and will fight
Until as any one we're free.
    And can enjoy our every right.

For is this not our native land?
    Have we not toiled for this our home
And bled, and made as brave a stand
    In its defense as e'er was known?

We've no more rapists, thieves and crooks,
    Nor do more crime, than other folks;
We love as well our arts and books
    And labors; we despise the yoke

Of bondage, ignorance and vice;
    We are as Christian in our deeds;

And naught can our demand suffice
   Which less than fullest rights concedes.

I know not why, because of race,
   We should be shunned, proscribed, despised
By those who, though of lighter face,
   Are yet our kindred by the ties

Of creed, of native land, and blood.
   I know not why we should pay tax
For government and yet a flood
   Of senseless protest—these are facts—

Should rise throughout our land's extent
   When we demand a voice and part
In offices of government;
   Such acts are tyrannous at heart.

The Negroes of the Southern state
   Who are denied the right to vote,
To have a court adjudicate
   Their wrongs, though stars and stripes do
     float

Above their heads, are treated worse
   Than were the subjects of the crown
Before rebellion moved the curse
   And shot the tyrant's army down.

Shall we, who know no other home,
    Who speak the native English tongue,
Submit to wrong without a groan
    And leave a serf's lot to our young?

No!   We shall not.   Not even beast
    Will be abused without a show
Of protest.   We must be released;
    We must strike some decisive blow.

If we betray our fathers' trust
    Bequeathed to us upon their death
In civil war, may our base dust
    Receive but curse from human breath.
*Dec., 1907.*


## A MEMORIAL OF CHILDHOOD.

Those days of childish thought and joy
    Will never come to me again,
Yet, there's no power that can destroy
    Their image drawn by mem'ry's pen,

Those days of innocence and love
    When I knew nothing of the world
Have flitted from me like a dove;
    Life has its graver scenes unfurled.

Those happy days at grandma's knee
    When I was but a tottering babe
No more can I expect to see,
    For long has she to rest been laid.

I knew no sorrows then, nor cares,
    For mother for me bore them all
And taught me of the hidden snares,
    Lest I might blindly in them fall.

No more will grandpa bring me sweets
    And trinkets when he comes from work;
No more shall I run out to meet
    My papa in my clean, new skirt.

Those days are gone, and in their place
    Are months of toil and years of hope,
But I am strengthened in life's race
    By drinking from the springs they ope.
*Dec., 1907.*


## A NOVEMBER EVENTIDE.

### (Published in the Willistonian.)

[Written on a Trolly Car.]

The mighty sun had kept his steady course
    Across the autumn sky of cold, steel gray,

Before him routing all the frosty chill
   And spreading o'er the earth a cheerful  day,

And was about to set him down to rest,
   To dream of all the  hearts  he'd  filled  with
      light
And leave the silver visage of the moon
   To rule o'er his dominion through the night,—

For Luna was his sweetheart, loved of old,
   Reflected from himself and fashioned, too,
Yet, fairer than his ruddy face of gold,
   She took upon herself a silver hue.

But ere he'd finished quite his daily run,
   His pale companion raised her silvery head
From 'neath the rugged top of Nonotuck
   And smiled, and great Sol blushed a crimson
      red.

Still higher rose the goddess of the night,
   Her full, bright smile o'erspreading wood and
      field:
Still lower sank her lover in the west
   Until Mt. Pomeroy his blush concealed.

But Luna steered her course across the sky
   And in his footsteps,  laughing,  held  the
      chase,

While here on earth, more fortunate than she,
  Sweet Morpheus held the world in loved em-
    brace.

*Nov., 1907.*


## MEMORIAL DAY IN EASTHAMPTON.

[Written for The Enterprise, Easthampton, Mass.]

'Twas kind of the Omnipotent
  To blow His warm breath on the day
And keep the rain in heavens pent,
  That we in duty sad might lay

Our decorations on the tombs
  Of heroes of our cruel wars.
The sun shone forth in splendid gloom;
  With drooping heads the trees and flowers

Stood still in thankful prayer, or raised
  Their joyful faces toward the heaven
Exulting gratefully in praise
  For all the goodness to us given.

No rain-cloud marred the clear, blue sky,
  No wintry blast the wind congealed

138

While white-haired heroes waved on high
　The tattered flags from battle-field.

The fifers piped the shrill war note,
　Or played the solemn funeral dirge;
A feeble step marked each drum stroke;
　A feeble heart each life did urge

As to their comrades' graves they went,
　Each with the weight of old age bent,
To pay with laurel wreaths and flowers
　A nation's debt of thanks.　'Tis ours

To mourn those hearts which valor claimed,
　To shed tears o'er those graves unnamed,
To cheer these heroes with us yet,
　Lest their great service we forget.

'Tis ours to soothe their feeble ills
　Whose memory each true heart fills:
'Tis ours, when they are passed and gone,
　To take their flag and follow on;

And as God gave a day so clear,
　So warm, from out this spring so drear,
That we might better pay respect
　To those deceased whose graves we  decked,

So will our later days be bright,
　Though weighed with years, our spirits  light,

Because we have revered the gray
  Old heroes on Memorial day.
*June, 1907.*


## PLEA OF THE NEGRO SOLDIER.

("A Powerful Poem and Foreboding"—Republican.)

[Published in Springfield Republican, Feb. 16, 1907. Copied
by Boston Guardian.]

America, ungrateful land!
  Whose treacherous soil my blood  has  dyed,
Whose wealth my father's shackled hand
  Has hoarded up, who has denied

Me right to live, to vote, to learn,
  Whose laws protect me not from wrong,
Who will permit me not to earn
  An honest living, who in song

Doth boast a land of freedom, but
  Whose flag waves o'er a land of crime,
The makers of whose laws unjust
  Themselves are stained with blood and  slime

Of murders, lynchings, rape and lies,
  And who, while yet the sacred oath

Of office on their vile lips lies,
    Will lead a mob of comrades forth

To take some negro, innocent,
    Accused perhaps, but never tried,
From custody of government
    And burn him, to a pillar tied,

I fear the dawning of thy doom:
    I hear the voice of justice cry
From out this wilderness of gloom:
    I see the dark clouds in thy sky.

From Boston massacre, my blood
    Through all the channels of thy war
Has mingled with thy crimson flood;
    Through Yorktown, Erie, Wagner,—far

To El Caney and San Juan Hill,
    Where, midst the charges awful din,
With song our voice the air did fill
    And make that song a battle hymn.—

The Philippines, so dearly bought,
    Are strewn with bodies of my kin;
My comrades have thy glory wrought
    In war, in peace, with skill and vim.

'Twas I who rescued from the urn
    Of death thy fickle soldier chief;

Tis he who gives me in return
  Disgrace, dishonor, no relief

From poverty my feeble years
  Must bring me soon; he who deprives
Me of support retirement rears
  Up for her faithful soldiers' lives.

My thirty years of living death
  In bloody war avail me naught
When prejudice and perjured breath
  Of Brownsville 'gainst my name is brought.

And dost thou yet, ungrateful land
  Expect my blood and kin to stand
In cowered silence, while thy hand
  Continues to despoil our band?

May God forbid that of my race
  A single child shall e'er disgrace
His native land, the resting place
  Of martyred kin, by fear to face

Injustice by whomever thrown.
  The ancient Plebeians of Rome
For treatment such renounced their home
  And sought the Sacred Mountain's dome.

The colonies of George the Third
  To less injustice war preferred

And fired,—the while the world concurred,—
  The shot which round the earth was heard.

Republic cannot long endure
  When autocrat can feel secure
To heap injustice on the poor
  Or helpless; ruin follows sure.

Three centuries have near rolled by
  Since first our fathers' mournful cry
And clank of chains rose to thy sky,
  Nor yet have found just cause to die.

Our voice of protest shall not cease
  Until thy unjust bonds release
Our rights, that our lives may increase
  In riches, happiness and peace.

  But I, alas! have given all
  In answer to thy urgent call,
  Exposed my life to sword and ball,
  And now, as o'er me creeps the fall

  Of life, I find no recompense
  But base discharge, with no defense
  Through which to prove my innocence,
  Though I've committed no offense.

  For this I've given up my home
  O'er hapless battle-fields to roam,

I've crossed the ocean's hungry foam,
I've fought disease in hostile loam.

O God of justice and of right!
If thou art deaf and hast no sight,
Lend me Thy weapons and Thy might,
That this last battle I may fight.
*Feb., 1907.*


## MEDITATIONS OF A NEGRO'S MIND. VI.

Justice, hast thou fled and left us
    In this cuel, unkind land,
Where these human wolves beset us
    As we turn on either hand?

Reason, hast thou taken refuge
    In some distant, kinder clime,
Leaving us in all this deluge
    Of unjust, uncivil crime?

Mercy, art thou deaf, unflinching
    To our hopeless wails and woes
As we're burned and killed by lynching,
    Murdered by our hideous foes?

Christian, has thy heart, once tender,
    Hardened into dead, cold stone:
Canst thou not some service render,
    Or dost thou these wrongs condone?

Conscience, art thou dreaming, sleeping,
    Nor reprovest thou these deeds?
Civil progress, art thou creeping
    Back into uncivil weeds?

Pride, art thou o'erwhelmed and blinded
    By false prestige, power assumed?
Take heed lest thou be reminded
    Suddenly that thou art doomed.

Where is all the honor boasted,
    Freedom, principle and right,
Written, sung, proclaimed and toasted
    Of this land of wealth and might?

Whittier's dead and Lincoln, Sumner,
    Garrison and Lovejoy, Stowe,
Phillips, Brown and Douglass slumber,
    While the pleas of "Fighting Joe,"

Keifer, Garrison, the younger,
    Higginson, and others few,
Still are scorned, unquenched of hunger,
    Yet to justice they are true.

145

Wisdom, hast thou lost thy power
  To convince the ignorant
That as they misuse thy dower
  They must certainly repent?

Woe unto this haughty nation
  If she fails to keep her trust:
All are equal by creation;
  All alike return to dust.
*Dec., 1907.*


## TO CHICAGO.

Chicago, mistress of the lakes,
  Controller of our inland trade,
The freest city of our states,
  What wondrous strides thy fame has made!

The century has yet one-fourth
  Its years to register with time
Since from an humble Negro's hearth
  Thou started on thy upward climb;

From farm to Indian trading-post,
  To Dearborn's fort, to thriving town,
To city, till now thou canst boast
  Of prestige, glory and renown.

146

When dreadful fire laid waste thy land
　　Thy courage took a deeper drill
And sank its roots beneath the sand,
　　And since that time has said, "I will."

As if from magic rose thy blocks
　　Like mountains towering to the skies;
The lake birds crowded to thy docks;
　　And o'er thy arms of steel and ties

Came people, money, shops and mills,
　　Came grain and livestock; 'cross thy plain
Came wagons from the eastern hills;
　　And from the South, to breathe again

The air of freedom and of life,
　　Came sons of Africa, escaped
From chains of slavery's deadly strife,
　　And drank the pure air of the lake.

Oft since Fred Douglass thou hast heard,
　　A Ransom shielded with thy walls,
A Morris hast thou given birth;
　　Another Morris filled thy halls

With melodies and music sweet.
　　Abe Lincoln, once, oft came and went
From hall of statehouse to thy street:
　　And now a Douglass settlement

Has graced thy great community,
  Has hurled its challenge through the land,
Determined with impunity
  For equal rights to all to stand.

A Justice Harlan is thy son,
  A Celia Parker Woolly, thine,
A Marshall Field,—whose race is run,—
  And many of illustrious line.

Thou city of an Indian swamp,
  My second birth thou gavest me:
As through thy long streets I did romp
  I breathed thy spirit deep and free.

From thee I learned my lessons first
  Of worldly care, of manly strife;
From thee I partly quenched my thirst
  For knowledge and the greater life.

I've wandered through thy groves and parks,
  Thy boulevards and avenues;
I've watched the sailing of thy barks
  And mingled with the busy crews;

I've seen thy buildings rent with fire;
  I've seen thy towering structures rise,
Each vieing to extend the higher,
  In climbing upward toward the skies.

148

Thou city on a sand-bar made,
  I've seen thy wealth and people grow
To double in one short decade;
  I've felt thy piercing, cold winds blow;

Oh city of the pioneer,
  I love thee for thy great, free heart;
Thou art my foster-mother, dear,
  And I am of thyself a part.
*Dec., 1907.*


## HAPPINESS IS HEAVEN.

### (To a Friend.)

[Written in a Music Lover's Calendar.]

When music rises sweet from harmony
And steals her soothing strains throughout
    my soul
And swells its living veins of melody
Until, sublime with ecstasy, they burst
Into a flood of joy, exuberance
And life subduing discord, sorrow, strife,
Then truly am I in the only heaven
That can exist for carnal, mortal man;
For harmony is but the voice of love,
And love is but a sympathetic chord

Of feeling which itself attaches to
The kindred particles of different
Existing organisms and binds them fast
Into sublime, harmonious happiness,—
Securest state of pleasure grown from life:
Therefore is love the leveler of life.
The soul compounded is of life and love,
The one true state of life is consciousness
Of happiness in other beings near
Resulting largely from one's own good deeds;
And, as the rhythmic utt'rance of the soul
Is poetry, so, therefore, music the
Denominator common is of life.
Since heav'n consists of  music, life, and  love,
Our only heaven, then, is happiness.
*Dec., 1907.*

## A HERO'S DEED.

A southern mob upon a lynching bent,
   In old Louisiana's slave-shorn bound,
With  murd'rous  hands  and  flaming firebrands
     went
   In lawless chase to hunt a negro down.

Our hero kissed farewell his child and dame,
  And  bravely  vowed  to  fight  their  coward
    band:
His eye possessed a never-failing aim
  And steady as yon mountain was his hand.

He knew that they were coming for his life,
  So, barricading windows all and doors,
And with his guns all loaded for the strife,
  He lay in wait for their approach  by  scores.

When  they  had  reached  and  turned  into  his
    gate
  He  fired  a  shot  which  struck  the  foremost
    down,
And  as  he  fired  he  prayed  he  might  shoot
    straight,
  That  every  shot  should  bring  one  to  the
    ground.

At this they made a rush toward his fort,
  But his good weapons were of truest steel,
So every bullet sailed into its port,
  And soon some eight or  ten  had  ceased  to
    feel.

They started back in horror at his deeds,
  For they were all base cowards, every one;

Some tried to sneak up nearer through the
    weeds,
    But even they did not escape his gun.

They tried all kinds of schemes to get him out;
    They sent a priest and small child toward
        the door,
But our black hero aimed his rifle stout,
    And both fell wounded gravely, streaked with
        gore.

He knew his God was with him in the fight
    And, therefore, could not be in e'en the priest;
He fought because he knew that he was right;
    And thirteen of the mob their blood re-
        leased.

But finally, by throwing oil and brands,
    They set the house afire to burn him 'live
And chuckled 'mong themselves and wrung
    their hands,
    For they thought no escape he could con-
        trive.

Quite soon the shanty was a mass of flames;
    The rifle ceased to speak; there were no
        tones
Except the crackling of the wood and panes:
    The fiends were waiting 'round to mock his
        groans.

But, while they stood intently looking on,
    The God of Mercy came and succor gave,
For, while they watched the house burn, he had
      gone:
    The flame and smoke refused to kill the
      brave.

The fire sent forth a heavy cloud of smoke
    To make the hero covering to the wood,
The wind obeyed the flaming tongue that spoke
    And wrapped his fleeting form in that dense
      hood

Until the dismal swamp stretched forth her arm
    And, covering him with her verdant shawl,
Fast wafted him beyond the reach of harm
    And left him north of Mason-Dixon's wall.

In vain they hunted, when the fire had died,
    To find his simmering bones, or ashes gray;
In vain they wondered where he could have
      hied
    Himself unseen to cheat them of their prey.

But this brave black had made good his escape;
    The fierce beasts even hindered not his
      flight;
Sweet Nature did his thirst and hunger sate
    And shield him with her cloak both day and
      night.

The mighty power that our fate controls
    Had spoken and rebuked the dastard mob;
Had sacrificed a dozen hateful souls
    To save one guiltless of a race down-trod.
*Dec., 1907.*


## CONSOLATION.

[Written in an Autograph Album, to M. E. G.]

Although at times our spirits seem oppressed
And we seem lonely, sorrowful, distressed,
We may find consolation, after all,
By turning t'ward the pictures on the wall:
So, if you find yourself in lonely pain,
Remember, sunshine always follows rain,
Then turn you to my humble photograph
Upon the wall, or to this autograph,
And fancy there my spirit and my soul
And it, perhaps, your heartache will condole.
*Nov., 1907.*

# AS WE LOVE, SO ARE WE LOVED.

[To M. E. G.]

Though the soil be e'er so fertile,
　It will not yield up its fruit
If no showers fall upon it,
　If no warmth caress its root.

Though the bud be near to bursting,
　It will not its beauty show
If no moisture fall upon it,
　If no sunlight lend its glow.

Though the heart be all affection,
　It will not its soul outpour
If no fervor be returned it,
　If no love knock at its door.

Just a word of loving kindness,
　Just a gentle look, or act
In our life, our talk, our writing
　May another's love attract.

If we wish to reap love's harvest,
　We must shed our hearts' warm rain
Of encouragement upon it,
　Or our sowing is in vain.

*Dec., 1907.*

155

# OUR RECOMPENSE.

Our lives are the sweeter because we have sor-
    rowed;
  Our love is more tender because we have
    pined;
Our sympathy deeper because we have suf-
    fered;
  Our happiness greater because we are kind.
*Jan., 1908.*


## TO WILLISTON AT PARTING.

### (Dedicated to Dr. Joseph H. Sawyer.)
[Published in the Willistonian.]

O Williston, a countless debt I owe
  To thee who hast assisted me in life,
For when my eager zeal desired to know,
  To do, when lone my heart, engulfed in strife,

For knowledge cried, for opportunity,
  For equal right and chance to live and learn,
To educate myself and happy be
  Though poor, proscribed, thou badst me come
    and earn

That lore, nor didst deny me of thine aid.
  Thy heart is great and good, ordained of
    God:

Thy tribute have already hundreds paid
  Unto thine ear and passed beneath the sod;

And some are marching feebly to the strains
  Of that sweet rhythm of life they learned of
    thee
As in their youthful days they coursed thy lanes
  Of learning, while full grateful at thy knee

Bow I, that thy wise benediction may
  In parting fall upon my storm-tossed head,
That thy good wish may pave my hard, rough,
    way
  O'er thorn, o'er wall, o'er grave of hallowed
    dead.

And when o'er western plain or eastern hill
  I hear thy loving voice in later years
Speak words of cheer and courage to me, still
  My grateful heart shall lend thee eager ears;

My tender mem'ries shall their petals ope
  And show thee there the full bloom of their
    soul
And breathe their fragrant, sunny breath of hope
  And joy into thine air;—and then, the goal.
*Jan., 1908.*

# LOUISE.

Can I forget your loving mien, Louise?
　　Can I forget your tender, trustful heart?
Can I forget your sacrificing soul?
　　Ah no!　They are of memory a part.

Have I not grateful seemed unto your mind?
　　Then think not of our meeting with regret,
For I have often thought of you, although
　　Some years have rounded now since we have
　　　met.

Your noble, quadroon face, your pretty eyes,
　　Your ruddy cheeks, your wavy, chestnut hair,
Your stately form, your womanly deport,
　　And e'en the music of your voice, are there

Among the pictures of my galleried mind,
　　Shut up within its chambers, to await
My pleasure to release them to my view,
　　My hungry turning toward the past to sate.

I feel that this I owe to you, Louise,
　　For you are yet the dear friend of my youth
Whose kindness and devotion shall not pine
　　For lack of recognition and of truth.
*Jan., 1908.*

## WOMAN.

Thou, woman, art a jewel of great worth
  And yet a worthless jewel if thou wilt:
Thou hast a value rarest of the earth,
  But thou art valueless when set in guilt.

*Jan., 1908.*


## THE BIRDIE THAT HAS FLOWN.

### [To a Friend.]

A birdie entered in our hall one day
  In dainty, sparkling plumage decked, with
    cheek
Of rosy pink and pretty eyes.   Straightway
  She glided t'ward my humble station meek

And perched herself in comfort on my chair.
  And when she oped her mouth and spoke to
    me
Her voice, so sweet and musical and rare,
  Fell on my ear and lingered, and so free

Did she present me from her silver purse
  Of treasure that for joy my heart-beat leaped
And listened to the song she did rehearse
  Into my ear inclined; and as she peeped

Into my face with sparkling, smiling eyes
  Her heart seemed smitten with my pleasant
    mien
And poured its story forth without disguise
  As I a dainty morsel for this queen

Set down upon the table at my side.
  And when her hunger she had fully quenched
She chirped good-bye, then straight without she
    hied,
  And next day came again unto my bench.

And daily as I waited in the hall,
  She came and chatted with me in delight
And left her pleasant treasure, soul and all,
  That I might dream the sweeter through the
    night.

  But now my bird has flown away and gone
  To cheer some other suitor with her lay
And left me but the echoes of her song
  To cheer my lonely musings of the day.
*Jan., 1908,*

# IS MACBETH A "GOD IN RUINS?"

[Written as an Exercise in English, at Williston.]

A god, Macbeth?    No he is not a god,
Nor demigod; though hero still he be,
He hath no deed to deify performed
That's not o'erbalanced by some fiendish act,
Some dev'lish deed by wicked greed set on.
Unholy rev'rence of ambition's call
Hath robbed him of his virtue's saner self,
Dethroned his God-like qualities of heart
And crowned instead a grim, Satanic head
With blasted, evil, fame-shorn boastful and
Unhallowed glory of a murd'rer's lot:
And yet, he hath a tender, kinder strain
Which doth betimes express its manly self
And seek to overpower its counterpart
Of dark desire, but that she demon of
His earthly tie, that gentle creature turned
To cold, dead stone, also ambition's child,
Unholy in her base desire for name,
Unsexed by evil passion's claim of power,
Unseats his reason from its holy throne
And places there instead to rule his fate
The maddened fury of his baser wish;
And Macbeth's mortal god of right falls dead.

*Jan., 1908*

# WILLISTON BATTLE SONG.

[Published in the Willistonian.]

Two football teams met one day
Down on the gridiron gay,
One wore the colors to "Worcester" true,
Red and black, as they flew
Out to fight Gold and Blue.
Proudly they ran to the field,
Cheered by the crowd as they wheeled,
But ere the game was done
With dear old Williston
They were compelled to yield,

CHORUS—

    Let us give a hearty cheer
    For old Williston so dear
    And for all her sturdy men
    Winning laurels for old "Sem."
    May they ever play so well
    That our spirits rise and swell,
    Let us all join in a rousing, good yell!
    Williston! Rah! Rah! Rah! Williston!
        Rah! Rah!

After the battle was o'er
"Worcester" went home worn and sore;
Williston cheered for the Blue and Gold
While the chapel bell tolled,

And the bonfire smoke rolled.
So may we always in strife,
Whether in school or in life,
Ever play fair and in
All of our struggles win
Williston fame and pride.
*Oct., 1907.*


## THE LATENT THOUGHT.

There is no heav'n such as we're told
With marble halls and streets of gold,
Where angels wing their joyous flight,
Where all are clothed in robes of white.

There is no hell of burning stone
Where wicked souls forever groan
And burn,—nor lives a devil there—
Where all is darkness and despair.

Our conscience is the god we serve;
Our every act it does observe;
Our thoughts originate within
It, and we're turned by it from sin.

The devil is no more nor less
Than mem'ry of our wickedness

Ambitious, covetous desire
Of all its servants does require.

Our happiness is all our heaven;
It is of life the one sweet leaven;
Remorseful misery is our hell;
It is of life the solemn knell.

Our highest aim while life remain
Should be to stop some others' pain,
To do as we would have them do;
To make them happy, love them, too;

For life is gone when last we breathe;
We live no more when this we leave;
And as we live in joy or fear,
We have our hell or heaven here.

If we do good but for the pay
We're offered "of eternal day;"
If we do naught but what is right
For fear of hell's eternal night;

We are unworthy of reward—
We should do good for sweet accord—
And we are moral cowards all.
If we do good, whate'er befall,

In order that because we live
The world may better be and give

Us joy because we've made it so,
No greater should we wish to know;

For Heaven is a state combined
Of music, joy and love refined,
And all these hover round our soul:
If we but try, we reach the goal.

So, if you would in Heaven be,
Do good, be happy and be free;
But if to wickedness you're slave
You'll enter hell before the grave.
*Feb., 1908.*


## SHAKESPEARE MODERNIZED.

Who lynches me maims but this modeled clay;
And injures no one but his narrow self,
Although in principle he wrongs a race,
For souls of martyrs have eternal life;
But he who robs me of my all, my name,
Steals that which cannot make him wealthier,
But slanders me and leaves me poor indeed.
*Feb., 1908.*

## MEDITATIONS OF A NEGRO'S MIND. VII.

The same air purifies our blood,
The same food gives us health and  strength,
The same stream quenches all our thirst,
All our emotions are the same,
Our minds imbibe the self-same thought,
Our feelings wounded are the same,
Sweet nature yields our toil as much,
The flowers bloom for us as well,
We're born, we live, we die the same,
When we are dead the self-same sod
Receives our bodies, and our souls
Are happy in the heaven, as yours,
'Tis true that our complexion is
Not light of color as is yours,
But should we, thefore, be proscribed
And ostracised, and scorned, and wronged?
*Feb., 1908.*


## TO ONE UNKNOWN.

To one unknown to me,
A lady, kind and good,
Of old New England stock,
Who saw I loved to read,—

Once on a western train,—
And bought for me a book,
Although she knew me not,
I now indite these lines.

There are some few great hearts
Who have compassion for
A struggling, outcast race,
Whose sympathies are moved
And touched with pity deep
To see a worthy one,
Deprived of equal chance,
Still strive to raise his state;—
And she was one of them.

Some years have passed since then,
But I have not forgot
Her kind and generous act.
Here in this rhymeless verse
A grateful, proud heart sings
His lay of thankful praise
Unto an unknown grace
And bids the silent breeze
To waft his song to her
And whisper in her ear
That it was not in vain
She did an act so kind.

*March, 1908.*

# A LOVER'S PROPOSAL.

My dear, sweet girl; I fancy you
Because you seem sincere and true:
   Because you seem in thought so pure;
Because you have an aim in life;
Because you've suffered want and strife;
   Because you suffer naught to lure
You from the work you've planned to do:
For Orpheus you've set to woo.

I like you for your honest face;
Your earnestness and easy grace.
   I care not for mere outward show
Of features, for 'tis but a thin
Veneering;—lifeless, bloodless skin.
   I find more beauty in the glow
Of fervency and love and truth
That lights your face and tints your youth

Than in the facial handsomeness
Of many girls who primp and dress
   And spend their time in idle talk;
Who can do nothing well but be
Much talked of in "society;"
   Whose greatest pleasure is to mock,
Or imitate some foppish flirt,
To wear the finest hat or skirt.

True beauty dwells within the soul,
And only there.   The face is cold
    Without expression's tints and fires:
'Tis but the mirror of the heart,
Reflecting life's most studied art,
    Portraying feelings, thoughts, desires
And longings, agonies and pain,
The unassuming and the vain.

The training of your girlhood days
Is well defined in all your ways:
    You could not hide it if you would.
It well becomes you to obey,
To reverence your mother's gray.
    I like you, for I think you're good.
I wonder if I'd ever rue
It, should I fall in love with you.

To satisfy me, I shall say
That, if, in future, day by day,
    Your life and acts continue to
Be worthy as I think you now
To be, I'll make a solemn vow
    That I shall love and honor you
And trust you with my name and fate.
If you will but reciprocate.
*April., 1906.*

# ONLY THE SPAN OF A LIFE.

[To Mrs. J. K. P.]

Only the span of a life has passed
    Since we were two little girls
Romping and playing, with ne'er a care,
    Finding but joy in our worlds.

Only the span of a life has gone
    Since we knew nothing of pain:
After a few more of life's frail days
    We shall be painless again.

Only a space of three score and ten,
    Filled with some joy with some strife;
Leavened with faith, hope, ambition, love,
    Makes up what we call a life.

Only the memoirs of childhood days
    Flit through our worn, weary brain
And, as we dream of our happy youth,
    Lo! We are children again.

But, as if shadows, they fly away,
    Back to their long-guarded cell,
There to continue their romp and play
    Till life responds to death's knell.

Only the span of a life has passed,
　　But we have not lived for naught,
For we can go to our graves at last
　　Happy for what we have wrought.
*May, 1906.*

## OUR AIM IN LIFE.

We all should endeavor to make others happy,
　　For life of itself enough sorrow will give:
Our sympathy, happiness, love, all have value—
　　The world should be better because we have
　　　lived.
*May, 1908.*